NOTES ON SONTAG

WRITERS ON WRITERS

ALSO BY PHILLIP LOPATE

ESSAYS

Being with Children

Bachelorhood

Against Joie de Vivre

Portrait of My Body

Totally Tenderly Tragically

Waterfront: A Walk around Manhattan

Rudy Burckhardt: Life and Work

Getting Personal: Selected Writings

FICTION

Confessions of Summer

The Rug Merchant

Two Marriages

POETRY

The Eyes Don't Always Want to Stay Open

The Daily Round

EDITED ANTHOLOGIES

Journal of a Living Experiment: The First Ten Years
of Teachers & Writers Collaborative

The Art of the Personal Essay: An Anthology
from the Classical Era to the Present

Writing New York

American Movie Critics: An Anthology
from the Silents Until Now

PHILLIP LOPATE **NOTES ON SONTAG**

PRINCETON UNIVERSITY PRESS

Princeton and Oxford

Published by Princeton University Press, 41 William Street,
Princeton, New Jersey 08540

In the United Kingdom: Princeton University Press, 6 Oxford
Street, Woodstock, Oxfordshire OX20 1TW

Library of Congress Cataloging-in-Publication Data
Lopate, Phillip, 1943–

   Notes on Sontag / by Phillip Lopate.

      p. cm. — (Writers on writers)

   ISBN 978-0-691-13570-0 (cloth : acid-free paper)

1. Sontag, Susan, 1933–2004—Criticism and interpretation.

2. Women and literature—United States—History—20th
century.   3. United States—Intellectual life—20th century.
I. Title.

   PS3569.O6547Z76 2009

   818'.5409—dc22   2008041120

British Library Cataloging-in-Publication Data is available

This book has been composed in Minion Pro with Myriad Pro

Printed on acid-free paper. ∞

press.princeton.edu

Printed in the United States of America

10 9 8 7 6 5 4 3 2 1

▣ LIST OF ABBREVIATIONS

BOOKS

AAIM	*Aids and Its Metaphors* (Picador, 1990)
AI	*Against Interpretation* (Dell, 1966)
ATST	*At the Same Time* (Farrar, Straus, and Giroux, 2007)
DK	*Death Kit* (Signet, 1968)
IA	*In America* (Farrar, Straus, and Giroux, 2000)
IAM	*Illness as Metaphor* (Picador, 1990)
IE	*I, Etcetera* (Vintage, 1979)
OP	*On Photography* (Farrar, Straus, and Giroux, 1977)
RPO	*Regarding the Pain of Others* (Picador, 2003)
SRW	*Styles of Radical Will* (Picador, 2002)

▣ INTRODUCTION

The Judgment

▣ For a writer to attempt a book about another writer, it requires nerve, some guild sympathy, and perhaps a dose of narcissistic projection. Also timing: when Ivan Bunin, who knew Chekhov, was asked after the older writer's death to do a biography of him, he hesitated. He waited almost fifty years, accruing nerve, writing his fiction, winning the Nobel Prize, until, at the brink of his own death, he composed a small book largely made up of questions about Chekhov and the unknowableness of any human being by another.

I cannot wait to win the Nobel Prize. The idea of one writer meditating on another holds enormous appeal for me, because we feed so much on each other's marrow. So when Princeton University Press, informing me of its intent to start a new series in which one writer would write about another, asked me which author I would choose were I to participate, I thought of Susan Sontag and immediately accepted. Her name popped into my mind because I had been recently mulling over the nature of her achievement and reputation. I had noted the curiously polarized critical responses she seemed to inspire: a tendency while she was alive to treat her with a deference bordering on awe, and, once she had died, to begin to disparage her. I counted myself in the middle: that is, I had always admired her as a writer, had been inspired by her essays particularly, though I often felt divided—loving one passage, not able to accept another—and this ambivalence struck me as a promising basis for a work of literary reflection. Had I chosen some writer whom I purely adulated, such as Montaigne or Hazlitt, I not only would have had to write on my knees, an awkward position, but I sensed I might have run out of things to say. My mixed feelings about Sontag would keep me indefinitely engaged. I could "stage" my ambiva-

lence, and work through it to some resolution—
or at least come to understand my own thought
processes better, the customary work of an essay.
If, as it has turned out, I sometimes seemed to be
taking back with one hand what I'd given with
another, the objectives I've tried to hold in mind
are balance, fairness, and honesty. Those who
are looking for a hatchet-job here will be as disappointed as those seeking hagiography.

The goal of objectivity has been complicated
by the fact that I knew Susan Sontag, however
slightly, over the years. We were acquaintances,
never forming either a friendship or an enmity.
The professional life of a mid-list writer is likely
to be punctuated from time to time by encounters
with literary luminaries who are far more famous
and celebrated, providing rich occasions for gratitude, resentment, or amusing memoir fodder, as
the case may be. I would like to think that my
encounters with the subject of this book have not
unduly colored my opinions of her written work.
My decision to write about these encounters—
that is, to introduce the word "I" into what is
otherwise largely a work of criticism, which may
strike some as unseemly—has to do with the fact
that I am trained as a personal essayist, but also
because I can't help hoping that by showing the
way Susan Sontag responded to situations in the

real world, it will bring some light to her persona on the page.

Of course the person one met in social situations and on the page were two different entities. She herself was quite conscious of this disparity, as when she wrote in an unusually self-analytical essay, "Singleness" (1995):

> Sometimes I feel I'm in flight from the books, and the twaddle they generate. . . . Oppressed by as well as reluctantly proud of this lengthening mini-shelf of work signed by Susan Sontag, pained to distinguish myself (I was a seeker) from her (she had merely found), I flinched at everything written about her, the praise as much as the pans. . . (that congeries of misunderstandings and stereotypes that make up one's reputation or fame). I'm not that image (in the minds of other people), it declares. And, with more poignancy, don't punish me for being what you call successful. I've got this onerous charge, this work-obsessed, ambitious writer who bears the same name as I do. I'm just me, accompanying, administering, tending to *that* one, so she can get some work done. (WSF, 260–61)

The problem with this plea was that she was not just a writer but a cultural celebrity, much-photographed, conjuring up instantly in the public's mind a certain physical form as well as an aura of mind, and that she herself had done much to shape, refine, and control that image of herself and cause it to proliferate. She needed attention, sought it, yet was shy at receiving it, feeling misunderstood—sometimes undervalued, sometimes overvalued, as if she had put one over on us. "My one perennial form of self-flattery: I know better than anyone what she is about, and nobody is as severe a judge of her work as I am myself" (WSF, 260).

One of the things that fascinates me about Sontag was her adapting one literary mask after another—the art critic, the polemical social policy advocate, the playfully wicked novelist, the war correspondent, and so forth—to express the full variety of her personality, all the while insisting on a rigid division between her self and her work. As she phrased it, "my books are not a means of discovering who I am, either; I've never fancied the ideology of writing as therapy or self-expression." (Interestingly, she did not always think so. In a 1961 diary entry she stated: "I write to define myself—an act of self-creation—part of the process of becoming—in a dialogue with writers I admire living and dead, with ideal readers.") However much she may have come to disdain the idea, inevitably her writing did become a means of self-discovery, possibly even self-healing, certainly self-consolation. In any case, here I am, a so-called authority on the personal essay, ruminating on someone who eschewed such personal essay writing, or did it only despite herself and usually through the medium of criticism. She was fiercely conscious of her uniqueness, convinced from the age of 3 or 4 that she was a genius, and kept searching for her peers or betters, dead or alive, to help convey those qualities, however much she came to deplore the vulgarities of self-expression. I want to trace here how she came to put forth the complicated identity of "Susan Sontag" over the course of her books, how she created this part-intentional, part-inadvertent persona, and to some extent became a prisoner of it, while at other times she was able to slip the knot of our expectations and augment her worldliness. The larger story is how any writer, starting with a range of interests and potentialities, comes, through variable deployment of those talents, to arrive at the patterns which delineate her achievements and limitations—her artistic fate.

Sontag was, like all of us, a creature of her times. She was also one of our foremost interpreters of the period through which she lived, our recent contemporary moment. In writing about her, I have found myself reliving with excitement and rue the same forty-plus years, and questioning the implicit assumptions that overhung these decades. What I am trying to say is that this book is not just my journey into Sontag-land, but my attempt to understand the slice of history we both shared.

One of Sontag's favorite structural devices was to organize her reflections around a set of notes. It was a technique that honored modernism's fragmentation and its modest disavowal of grand resolution. So I have taken her lead, and offer these "notes" on a fascinating literary figure. To be sure, while patterns are suggested, there is no single governing thesis that I am putting forth here, so don't bother looking for one. Instead, I have allowed myself the freedom to follow my nose, tracking some of Sontag's characteristic qualities, strategies, influences, enthusiasms, pet dislikes, and contradictions in an essayistic circling from different perspectives. By taking soundings, sometimes from a chronological, sometimes a thematic, sometimes a genre-oriented, sometimes a personal vantage-point, it is my hope that each will reinforce the others.

▥ According to Georg Lukacs, "The essay is a judgment, but the essential, the value-determining thing about it is not the verdict (as is the case with the system) but the process of judging." Interestingly, Sontag once wrote a cryptic diary entry to herself: "The greatest crime: to judge." While I intend in this book to take the reader through my own meandering process of judging Susan Sontag, perhaps it would be best to get the overall "verdict" out of the way first, to dispense with any false suspense.

Sontag's first three essay collections—*Against Interpretation, Styles of Radical Will, Under the Sign of Saturn*—constitute, to my mind, some of the enduring glories of American literary nonfiction. The brief I would make for them has nothing to do with whether her own opinions have stood up, but with the belief that her shorter essays are powerful constructions, eloquently argued, well-illustrated, often elegantly structured, and dense with suggestive, stimulating thought.

What is especially exhilarating about the essays in these first three collections is to be in the presence of her conviction. Whether you agree with her opinions scarcely matters; sometimes they are even more stimulating when you disagree, because she means to provoke. Part of their charm is that they gave us an exciting portrait of a new kind of woman: independent, open to pleasure, unencumbered by apologetic defensiveness about her intelligence.

Her diaries show that this conviction was partly a willed technique, a form of play-acting. In an entry dated Feb. 22, 1967, 3 a.m., she wrote: "I'm finishing the ['Story of O'] review which has turned into a 35-page essay. It's OK. Still, I don't believe a word I'm saying. It's interesting, maybe valuable—but I don't see how 'true'" (NYTM).

Her fiction is, in the main, poor. Maybe that's too harsh: her fiction is, for the most part, unsuccessful—the only exceptions being one novel, *The Volcano Lover*, which is lively and decent, and a few experimental short stories (such as "Unguided Tour" and "The Way We Live Now"). She lacked broad sympathy and a sense of humor, which are usually prerequisites for good fiction. More germane, perhaps, she did not convincingly command a fictive space on the page; her fiction seemed derivative, forced, studied; she was not a natural at staging and nurturing conflict, and would either shy away from plot or force it into melodrama. (Her films, with the exception of *Promised Lands*, have the same derivative, labored, unconvincing quality.) But what an essayist!

Is it comic or tragic, the way she came to undervalue her essay writing and insist she be honored for her novels, like the clown wanting to play Hamlet? Once, the Israeli writer David

Grossman approached her to say how much her essays had meant to him. "Bah! Have you read my *Volcano*?" She became touchy when people complimented her essays. Even in retrospect, when she wrote of the period that she composed the essays in *Against Interpretation*, she would only frame that time as the interval between her first novel and her second—a distraction from fiction. I, who revere the art of essay writing, and who can never regard literary nonfiction as even a fraction inferior to fiction, find puzzling Sontag's need to be thought primarily a novelist. But not unusual: postwar American writing featured a number of writers arguably better at nonfiction who preferred to be thought of as novelists: James Baldwin, Mary McCarthy, Gore Vidal, Norman Mailer, Truman Capote. Novels were considered the Big Game, essays the minor pursuit. In Sontag's case, there was more involved than status; there was something valiant about her need to reinvent herself. She had already succeeded as an essayist, and seemed to feel she had used up the problems of the form (or so she puts it in her foreword to a reissued edition of *Against Interpretation*).

Her fourth essay collection, *Where the Stress Falls*, may be too compendious, unfocused, a catch-all for her vagrant interests. Even so, it has remarkable pieces in it: the essays on Machado de Assis, Roland Barthes, and Robert Walser; the personal essays on travel; and her pieces on the choreographers George Balanchine, Merce Cunningham, and Lucinda Childs. Sontag wrote beautifully and knowledgeably about dance, which for her was a utopia of order and rapture, adhering to the highest standards of perfection, the consummate expression of her longing for "transparency." Overall, the overstuffed *Where the Stress Falls* is much underrated. Perhaps because she had already made such a point of wanting to be considered a novelist, the literary world took her too much at her word.

Her last, posthumous essay collection, *At the Same Time*, is her weakest. Her religion, in the end, came to be Literature. Certainly a worthy shrine, but the piety of these late essays is wearisome, as is the generality of her praise for literature, and her scolding stance that she is one of the last persons on earth who still loves books.

The declining quality of Sontag's late essays can be explained by a number of factors: illness may have taken their toll on her energy; she had transferred even more of her creative ambition to fiction writing, leaving essays an afterthought; the success of her earlier essays made it harder to top them—she would either need to reinvent the form, or coast; she had grown alienated from the dominant culture, no longer in step with its mood, and thus the pieces grew crabbier, exasperated, took on their scolding tone. Many later essays were prompted by occasions or the promise of a quick buck, as happens to all successful writers who become sought-after to write introductions to coffee table books, give award-winning speeches, present papers at international conferences—her article prose became more oral, more user-friendly, as well as more platitudinous and slack.

But, in fact, Sontag was never a consistent prose stylist. Some of her sentences are elegantly turned, others are clumsy and clotted. The inconsistency might have to do with the succession of masks she tried on, or with the variety of audiences she addressed. Always a hard worker, always in love with beauty, she herself did not have that automatic grace that certain writers of the highest order possess.

Her book-length essay projects—*On Photography*, *Illness as Metaphor*, *AIDS as Metaphor*, *Regarding the Pain of Others*—brought her a greater measure of popularity and renown. Passionately voiced, important books, which by her intellectual prestige alone turned the spotlight on the subjects they covered, they also seem to me attenuated, their arguments stretched to stridency, their initial promise left unrealized. Sontag was an aphoristic, compressed writer, and so it should be no surprise that she was at her best in shorter essays. She would weigh in, marching ahead with determination and force. By the end of twenty-five pages she had nailed it. When she spread out to the length of a book, the provocative, perverse nature of her arguments tended to fall apart. Once you had assimilated the moving, reasonable point that patients should not be victimized for their illnesses, there was nowhere else for *Illness as Metaphor* to go; the perverse, unreasonable part, which alleged that metaphors were bad for you, could never be wholly convincing, since the mind cannot work unmetaphorically. Of course her own prose in *On Photography* was wildly metaphorical: the camera was a gun, an instrument of violation, et cetera, and that indicting posture led to similar exaggerations.

Sontag did not, in the main, practice "thinking against oneself," as the Romanian essayist E. M. Cioran (about whom she wrote an admiring essay) recommended. She would customarily take a stand, charge in ferociously and at times sanctimoniously. She would not argue with herself within the borders of the essay, as many great essayists do; rather, she would take issue with herself in another, later piece of writing. Thus, "Fascinating Fascism" corrects her earlier defense of Leni Riefenstahl, and the straightforward humanism of *Regarding the Pain of Others* amends the prosecutorial zeal of *On Photography*, and "Questions of Travel," her essay on group jaunts to communist countries, administers a rebuke to her earlier naiveté in *Trip to Hanoi*.

In her posthumous collection of essays and speeches, *At the Same Time*, she often gave lip service to literature's need for skepticism and paradox, and claimed that "a good deal of my life has been devoted to trying to demystify ways of thinking that polarize and oppose" (ATST, 203). Actually, her demystifying was often in the service of opposition and polarization (though decades later she might occupy the opposite pole, equally forthrightly). There were a few times, however, when the poles of her ambivalence were allowed to stand inside the same text. Part of the allure of her most influential essay, "Notes on Camp," came from its ability to sustain an ambivalent, unresolved tone throughout. It is also her most purely aphoristic.

Sontag was the master of the aphoristic essay. She had the aphorist's disdain for qualifiers, such as "perhaps" or "occasionally," which might mar the sleekness of the quivering-arrow sentence hitting the bull's-eye. Here is how she wrote of the technique: "Most of the great aphorists have been pessimists, purveyors of scorn for human folly. . . . Aphoristic thinking is informal, unsociable, adversarial, proudly selfish" (USS, 191). In her hands, the blade cut both ways: her aphorisms could delight, but sometimes they came off as glib and did their author damage: for instance, "communism is Fascism with a human face."

She is often taken to task—and unfairly, I think—for having contradicted herself on certain matters, especially politics. I say "unfairly" because it can be a sign of growth and openness to change one's opinions. No, what is problematic is not that she contradicted herself over time, as everyone must, but that she kept taking strident, doctrinaire-sounding positions that did not seem to allow for the possibility that there were other, legitimate ways of thinking about the same topic—or the self-knowledge that she herself might come to them eventually. She was an enthusiast—a lover, not a skeptic—who needed to fall hard for a position and convince herself it was the only one.

"I am not at all interested in writing about work I don't admire," she told her *Paris Review* interviewer, Edward Hirsch. "And even among what I've admired, by and large I've only written about things I felt were neglected or relatively unknown. I am not a critic, which is something else than an essayist." Of course Sontag is a critic, and a valuable one, as well as an essayist; I take that last statement with a grain of salt. But she is following Auden (also a brilliant critic) in saying that life is too short to waste time reviewing books one doesn't think are any good. She is not a gate-keeper, turning away bad art. She is an enthusiast, calling our attention to the neglected gems we probably haven't noticed. When asked to name her favorite writer, she answered "Shakespeare," but since, as she explained, she felt she had nothing compelling or original to say about him, she did not bother to praise him in print.

In writing about those she admired, she may also have been establishing a literary lineage—to conclude in her. Nothing unusual about that: authors frequently cobble together, from their ancestors or contemporaries, a club of kindred spirits, in order to instruct the public how they wish to be considered. As she herself said, in her essay about Elias Canetti, who had paid a beautiful tribute to Herman Broch: "Such a tribute creates the terms of succession. When Canetti finds in Broch the necessary attributes of a great writer—he is original; he sums up his age; he opposes his age—he is delineating the standards to which he has pledged himself" (USS, 181). In her case, most of her standards and models were French and German.

She had a noisy quarrel with America. Yet she herself was very American: in her gift for self-invention; in her candor; in her dynamic, athletic recklessness; in her belief that hard work could transcend one's limitations. "Poor Susan," Barthes once told a friend of mine, Carlos Clarens. "She rows, she rows. . ." Meaning, I suppose: She tries so hard but she'll always lack that certain insouciant brilliance, such as he, her idol, had. In Barthes's disloyal, behind-the-back remark (she was ever loyal to *him*; he would greet her with "Ah Susan, *toujours fidèle*"), there was something of the European intellectual administering a rebuke to the dogged upstart American. Sontag herself said positively, using the very same metaphor: "Writing is, finally, a series of permissions you give yourself to be expressive in certain ways. . . . Allowing yourself, when you dare think it's going well (or not too badly), simply to keep rowing along" (WSF, 264).

Sontag insisted she was never bored. Even if true, she could get mighty impatient, which condition resembles boredom. She had an unequivocal disdain for the academy, insisting that it destroyed writers' souls (a view I would like to believe too sweeping). But she always kept up to date with literary theory, and her writing constantly signaled to academic readers that she was in dialogue with them. She managed to have it both ways: to embed shards of academic theory into her text, and to write clearly for a general public.

She often cultivated an elusive style, so that the general public had to run after her meaning with its tongue out, feeling stupid. She was both a popularizer and an obscurantist. She could be extremely direct, as any polemicist must; but she could also be opaque and hard to pin down, with her mastery of the impersonal mode. She was, for decades, the single most important bridge between intellectuals and the public. She also made a significant part of her living giving readings and lectures in short visits to universities. What was her beef, then, with academia? That it was populated with mediocrities, bores, overeager to win her approval? She loved parties, but academia was the wrong party.

She was a snob. To play the snob in American culture, with its chronic lip service to egalitarianism or leveling envy, is a tough act, and potentially a useful one. Sontag was snobbish the way certain star writers from the provinces are, who never lose the feeling of insecurity about their right to be seated on the dais, or their need to be so. For Sontag, there was an A-list and a Z-list and nothing in between. If you were not on the A list you were on the Z list, or the un-list, simple as that. Originally from Arizona and California, she was one of those Girls of the Golden West (along with Mary McCarthy, Pauline Kael, Joan Didion) who came east to New York, sometimes with a chip on their shoulders, to claim their spotlight.

She was courageous. She followed her son David to the battlefield of Savajevo. In intellectual battles, she was perfectly willing to take on conventional wisdom and make enemies. Yet it must be said that she was always positioning herself according to how she would be perceived by her peers or betters on the international stage; the need to be thought well of by the right people was apparently critical.

◫ In writing this book I have come to realize, sometimes uncomfortably, how much I have in common with my subject. I, too, have a habit of boasting, and a need to maneuver any situation so as to put myself in a superior light. I, too, get quickly impatient with ordinary chatter, tend to be detached, am something of a snob in aesthetic matters, and cherish the exquisite, neglected artwork. I, too, write essays and fiction, and am known more for the former than the latter (though, to me, that judgment seems entirely apt). It is a truism that we have a hard time tolerating in others the defects that reside in ourselves. I say all this by way of warning the reader to be armed with skepticism and argumentativeness for what follows. Mine is not meant to be the final word on this distinguished subject.

This book is not a biography (thank God), so I have not felt obliged to interview any relatives or close friends. What I have done, consistently, is to interrogate my own thoughts and feelings about Sontag. I view the result as primarily a conversation between two authors. Granted, one of them does not get to reply, but she had more than her say when she was alive. Eloquent as she was, I have had all I can do to hold up my end of the conversation. Whatever my reservations about Sontag may be, I notice that I am always talking to her in my head, she is always provoking me to think harder, her work stimulates me to reply, and that has made writing the book a joy. I would be less than honest if I did not admit that it also induced a fear that I would be punished for my hubris in taking the measure of such an intellectual icon. But I always had at hand the model of Sontag herself, the enthusiastic generalist who was unafraid to tackle any subject—and that has given me heart to persist.

⊞ NOTES ON SONTAG

Against Interpretation

🀫 As an essayist, Sontag began at the summit. *Against Interpretation* is one of the most impressive debuts in the history of American literary nonfiction. Having been a graduate student in philosophy, she took the high road by quoting Hegel and Nietzsche, and by advocating Cesare Pavese and Norman O. Brown, Robert Bresson and Jean-Luc Godard, while reconciling these difficult cultural figures with a taste for science fiction movies and camp. She spoke to the hunger for the new, freed from patriarchal probity. At the same time, she could be very shrewd, the smartest graduate student, the most filial daughter. Part of what gave these first essays of hers such impact was the way her opinions were utterly situated in the era's Zeitgeist.

For all the clichés now attached to the sixties, it *was* a special time in that people really seemed to believe that they were on the precipice of a new life. If, as Bob Dylan rudely put it, "Something is happening and you don't know what it is," Sontag was on hand to tell the aging *Partisan Review* crowd what exactly was happening, and what it meant—what to make, for instance, of "the close-ups of limp penises and bouncing breasts, the shots of masturbation and oral sexuality, in Jack Smith's *Flaming Creatures*" (AI, 226). Much of Sontag's conviction in her early prose comes from that context of idealistic ripeness; she spoke for and to a time that seemed ready to throw off the shackles of tradition, injustice, and repression. The word "liberation" crops up regularly in her first two essay collections, always as an unquestionable good. Then it disappears, around 1980, or becomes shaded by irony.

In her 1996 essay "Thirty Years Later . . ." she admitted: "I'm aware that *Against Interpretation* is regarded as a quintessential text of that now mythic era." After issuing various qualifications, such as that she is against packaging history into eras, and looks back on the decade mostly as a period when she wrote her two novels, as well as those essays that "had distracted" her from fiction, she goes on to defend the sixties by saying: "How marvelous it all does seem, in retrospect! How one wishes some of its boldness, its optimism, its disdain for commerce had survived. The two poles of distinctly modern sentiment are nostalgia and utopia. Perhaps the most interesting characteristic of the time now labeled the Sixties was that there was so little nostalgia. In that sense, it was indeed a Utopian moment" (WSF, 271).

She realizes, she goes on, that "the Sixties have been repudiated, and the dissident spirit quashed, and made the object of intense nostalgia," and rues what she sees as the present moment, an "age of nihilism." Yet, while loyal to the Sixties, her honesty forces her to consider that its irreverence may have planted the seeds for the undermining of seriousness, while "the more transgressive art I was enjoying would reinforce frivolous, merely consumerist transgressions." She stops well short of taking some of the blame herself for that unhealthy transformation—and indeed she should not have, since, even in her most approving affirmations of pop culture, pornography, and camp, there was a note of high seriousness in Sontag that could never pave the way for the merely frivolous. "In writing about what I was discovering, I assumed the preeminence of the canonical treasures of the past" (wss, 270). She was like a naughty teenager who tosses a rock at a school window to let in some fresh air, only to witness with horror the whole stately edifice crumble to the ground. Again, not that she was responsible for the triumph of pop culture over high culture—that was in the cards—but she must have felt baffled, if not a little guilty, at the collapse of high culture's prestige. "To call for an 'erotics of art' did not mean to disparage the role of the critical intellect. To laud work condescended to as 'popular' culture did not mean to conspire in the repudiation of high culture and its complexities" (wss, 272), she wrote testily.

As stated, Sontag had a nose for the topical, for the "new sensibility." This very topicality makes some of her pieces seem a little dated, mere literary journalism, but at the very least she was consistently able to diagnose the moment and prophesize the immediate future—which goes some way toward explaining her relevance as a public intellectual. Sontag articulated a cool perspective that spoke to youth. As she noted in a 1964 diary entry: "every age has its representative age group—ours is youth—spirit of age is being cool, dehumanized, play, sensation, apolitical." This sensibility, nowhere more evident than in films, the dominant medium of the time, was what excited us when *Breathless* came out, all those sassy jump-cuts and the Belmondo character's foolish daring. She became the spokesperson for youth's disgust with fuddy-duddy moralizing, and for a heightened attending, in a Wildean spirit, to the sensual surface and technique of a given work.

> Ours is a culture based on excess, on overproduction: the result is a steady loss of sharpness in our sensory experience. . . . What is important now is to recover our senses. We must

learn to *see* more, to *hear* more, to *feel* more.
Our task is not to find the maximum amount
of content in a work of art, much less to squeeze
more content out of the work of art than is
already there. Our task is to cut back content so
that we can see the thing at all. (AI, 13–14)

Her emphasis on style as morality was a necessary correction at the time. It also echoed a good
deal of the more advanced art and contemporary criticism. Willem de Kooning had said that
painting was about paint, and George Balanchine
declared that "Dance is just about dance." In his
1950's film criticism, Manny Farber had been
puncturing what he called "white elephant" art—
Oscar-winning, bloated, message pictures—
while praising the lean, unpretentious action
movies of Howard Hawks and Raoul Walsh;
in the 1960's Pauline Kael had been skewering
David Lean's *Ryan's Daughter* and other white
elephants and drawing attention to the erotics
of movie-going; meanwhile, Andrew Sarris was
busy citing examples to substantiate Andre Bazin
and the *Cahiers du Cinema* critics' thesis that a
film's innate morality could be deduced more by
its compositional framings, lighting, and camera movement than by any explicit speechifying.
Film buffs everywhere, captivated by the self-

reflective innovations of Godard, Truffaut, and Antonioni, shared the conviction that cinematic form was what counted. How impatient we got when a critic such as the *Times*' Bosley Crowther plodded through the treatment of some "daring" theme—pacifism or homophobia, say—in what we regarded as visually stodgy movies! Sontag spoke our language—or gave us the language in which to speak.

Sontag's basic orientation was that it is a wise idea to analyze a work of art's formal properties and maneuvers first, rather than trying to parse its symbolism or reduce it to an overall banality, such as society versus the individual. Her emphasis on the artistic process is actually in line with John Dewey's ideas in *Art as Experience*, though she would have never cited that Yankee educational philosopher as a source. If I tend to agree with her taste still, it may be because her aesthetic judgments have stood the test of time or because they've become so firmly anchored in my own worldview that I couldn't dislodge them if I tried. She will say, for instance, "Transparence is the highest, most liberating value in art—and in criticism—today. Transparence means experiencing the luminousness of the thing in itself, of things being what they are. This is the greatness of, for example, the films of Bresson and Ozu and

Renoir's *The Rules of the Game*" (AI, 13), and my first response is to echo "Hear! Hear!" Such pronouncements speak to an almost religious sense of art we share. If I press on the words hard, I start to wonder, What exactly is this "luminousness of the thing in itself, of things being what they are"? But then I think: Oh, you know what she means! And I have only to recall the many moments when the lamp in the background of an Ozu composition seemed to shine with a special illumination, suggesting the spirituality of objects at rest, or their volition, the way Bresson remarked, "Make the objects look as if they want to be there." I also agree with Sontag when she says, in her rich, thoughtful essay "On Style," that

> all great art induces contemplation, a dynamic contemplation. However much the reader or listener or spectator is aroused by a provisional identification of what is in the work of art with real life, his ultimate reaction—so far as he is reacting to the work as a work of art—must be detached, restful, contemplative, emotionally free, beyond indignation and approval. (AI, 27)

The emphasis on detachment over coercive identification is music to my ears. So, too, when she says "the moral pleasure in art, as well as the moral service that art performs, consists in the intelligent gratification of consciousness," at this fundamental level I am in total agreement with Sontag, that what makes art moral is a reorientation of our consciousness, rather than adherence to a checklist of whatever values are politically correct at the moment. Our disagreements, which I will address later, tend to proliferate at another level, having more to do with her eagerness to remain fashionable or "cutting-edge," which led her to dismiss rather too readily a few things I still hold dear, such as humanism, realism, and psychology.

In this first collection, Sontag defended camp and pornography, but she never lost sight of the fact that, whatever the satisfactions of "camp" taste, "an art of excess, lacking harmoniousness, can never be of the very greatest kind" (AI, 20). As for pornography, while she believed some of it (especially the French, self-conscious, "Story of O" kind) can qualify as art, she quoted Genet's statement that to the extent his works arouse readers sexually, "they're badly written, because the poetic emotion should be so strong that no reader is moved sexually. Insofar as my books are pornographic, I don't reject them. I simply say that I lacked grace" (AI, 27). And grace is all, in Sontag's cult of art. Sontag remains on some level a classicist, an Apollonian, embracing balance and harmony. Perhaps there is no contradiction here, like the teacher who writes on the blackboard in Godard's *Bande à Part*, "Classique = moderne." The point to remember is how often the younger Sontag pulled back from excess, how cautious and qualifying and reasonable she could be, having first staked out a doctrinaire position.

The "against" title she used in her essay is a time-honored strategy for marshalling polemical energy; and when the author's contrarian opposition rears up against a seemingly ineluctable good (such as Joyce Carol Oates's essay "Against Nature," Laura Kipnis's *Against Love*, or my own "Against Joie de Vivre"), there is an added frisson of throwing down the gauntlet to convention and common sense itself. To pretend to be against something which it is impossible truly to be against, either for practical or ethical reasons, is to conjure up a utopia, somewhere out of this world, and to open up a space for speculation, freedom, the breaking of taboos. Just as Sontag defends pornography, another quasi-utopian sphere beyond moral qualms or physical limits, so she dreams of a criticism shorn of interpretation—and for much the same reason, because it is sexy and liberating for her to think about.

"In place of hermeneutics we need an erotics of art," she famously asserted, in the last line of her "Against Interpretation." Certainly there were many precedents for this same desire: in Baudelaire; in Mallarmé, who called for a self-reflexive writing that would just be about writing; in Flaubert, who dreamed of a novel that was all plotless style; and above all, in the surrealists. These pure-style urges resurfaced in the sixties with a vengeance, curiously enough, in spite of its being such a politically active time. Partly a recurrence of the ideal of "art for art's sake," it yet held a political dimension: the revolutionary impulse that had crystallized in the New Left sought for a way to distance itself from the corny, moralizing agitprop of the Old Left.

Sontag, nobody's fool, was well aware that her call to reject interpretation made no sense on practical levels. As she wrote, decades later, in *AIDS and Its Metaphors*: "[O]f course, all thinking is interpretation. But that doesn't mean it isn't sometimes correct to be 'against' interpretation" (AAIM, 93). What is peculiar is that she maintained the zealot's posture while calling for impossibilities that she knew to be impossible. She simply put forward in deadpan her extremist demands. Advocating the avant-garde novel, she wrote: "Readers must be made to see, by a new generation of critics who may well have to force this ungainly period of the novel down their throats by all sorts of seductive and partly fraudulent rhetoric, the necessity of this move. And the sooner the better" (AI, 103). If there is comedy in this, it is the overheated comedy of all Futurist manifestos (think of Marinetti or Artaud) that invoke a too-strenuous ideal for ordinary humans such as the reader to follow, much less take seriously.

The truth is that, even at the time, Sontag did not argue that all interpretation was bad. There were historical moments, she noted, when certain types of interpretation could be liberating, as was the case with Marx and Freud. But our own era suffered, in her opinion, from a surfeit of interpretation, which stifled us and got in the way of our ability to experience the world head-on.[*] The paradox—it scarcely needs saying—is

---

[*] Roland Barthes showed a similar antagonism to verbal interpretation, writing that "the linguistic message no longer guides identification but interpretation, constituting a kind of vice which keeps the connoted meanings from proliferating. . . . With respect to the liberty of the signifieds, the text thus has a *repressive* value and we can see that it is at this level that the morality and ideology of a society are above all invested." Roland Barthes, "The Rhetoric of the Image," in Barthes, *Image/Music/Text* , trans. Stephen Heath (New York: Hill and Wang, 1977).

that she was relentlessly interpretative in her ferreting out the methods and motives of those who would place interpretation of content over formal description.

Against Interpretation is divided between hot polemics and sober appreciations. The title essay is a brilliant call to arms, "On Style" a further incitement: the essays on Pavese (the first in her portraits of male intellectual sufferers) and Simone Weil are balanced appreciations, demonstrating perspective and caution. She used manifestos to be outrageous, portraits to be judicious. Her essay on Camus is calm and fair, not a vicious attack, but a market correction. It begins with one of her opening-sentence categorizing gambits: "Great writers are either husbands or lovers." Camus turns out to be "the ideal husband of contemporary letters," but Sontag was not much drawn to husbands at that period in her life, so she brings him down a peg. Her Lévi-Strauss piece demonstrated that Sontag, while clearly aware of Structuralism, did not succumb to it, except in minor ways (such as her analysis of science fiction films, "The Imagination of Disaster"). She props up Georg Lukacs as someone who "has counted for a long time" before attacking him for being "crude" in his literary Marxism and insufficiently modernist, having preferred the "over-explaining"

Thomas Mann to Kafka. (Sontag herself had been in thrall to Mann as a teenager, a crush that later embarrassed her). She makes it clear she prefers Walter Benjamin to Lukacs, and the essay is in part a preparatory attempt to enthrone one by deposing the other.

In her 1964 essay, "Notes on Camp," included in *Against Interpretation*, she defends the importance of taste, and shows how a camp sensibility expands the realm of taste by arguing that "there exists, indeed, a good taste of bad taste" (AI, 291). Another way of putting this is, "The ultimate Camp statement: it's good because it's awful" (AI, 292). The essay thrives on paradox. In an uncharacteristically personal note, Sontag explains at the beginning that she has the right to define this phenomenon by virtue of her ambivalence: "I am strongly drawn to Camp, and almost as strongly offended by it. That is why I want to talk about it and why I can. For no one who wholeheartedly shares in a sensibility can analyze it; he can only, whatever his intention, exhibit it. To name a sensibility, to draw its contours and to recount its history, requires a deep sympathy modified by revulsion" (AI, 276). This requisite of "deep sympathy modified by revulsion" is a chancy one, especially as she goes on to connect camp sensibility with homosexual taste. Is she saying that she herself is partly revulsed by homosexuality? Certainly not, though she flirts with the idea, leaving it to die between the lines. So, too, does she omit to mention that she herself has had lesbian experiences. The essay derives its allure as much by the way it dances over to the edge of the abyss, looks down and skips back, as by anything it says. But she does have plenty of intriguing ideas: she links Camp to mannerist art, to the comic vision, to innocence, duplicity, the pathos of aging, to Wilde, to the artificial and unnatural, to the theatre. "Camp sees everything in quotation marks. It's not a lamp, but a 'lamp'; not a woman, but 'a woman.' To perceive Camp in objects and persons is to understand Being-as-Playing-a-Role. It is the farthest extension, in sensibility, of the metaphor of life as theatre" (AI, 280).

What is especially noticeable, alongside her brilliance, is her ambition. The piece begins with the taxonomical assertion: "Many things in the world have not been named; and many things, even if they have been named, have never been described." She will forthwith plant her flag on the territory of Camp, claiming herself as its first explorer. The piece appeared initially in *Partisan Review*, and was subsequently taken up and fussed over by news magazines of the day. During interviews decades later, Sontag professed to have been astonished by this public attention, claiming that her only ambition had been to write for a few thousand readers of intellectual quarterlies. In fact that is not entirely true: right before "Notes on Camp" was about to appear in print, she turned to a notable who was serving on a panel with her, and said excitedly, "I've just written a piece that is going to *put me over*."

And it did. More power to her. It makes me nostalgic for a time when a single essay could put anyone over.

Early Memories of Sontag

My first encounters with Susan Sontag occurred when I was an undergraduate at Columbia, between 1960 and 1964 and she was an instructor in the Religion Department. It did not take long to hear about this brilliant, dazzlingly attractive woman on the college faculty, who would come to be spoken of in the press as the intellectual's Natalie Wood. I remember seeing her at a Fair Play for Cuba rally, alongside the leather-jacketed, motorcycle-riding sociologist C. Wright Mills. Some of my friends were taking her Introduction to Religion course and reporting back to me the wonderful throwaway things she said: for instance, recommending that they attend a retrospective of Roberto Rossellini's films at the Museum of Modern Art. (I loved her for telling them that.) The Religion Department at Columbia back then was dominated by Jacob and Susan Taubes, a spookily thin, intense, attractive and super-smart couple. Jacob was supposed to be something of a holy man, a *zaddick*. Sontag seemed to be in thrall to this married couple (we undergraduates imagined them a threesome) who, even then, though perhaps I am reading back too much in hindsight, had a doomed aura about them: in the event, both died young, Susan Taubes by drowning herself. (Sontag would dedicate *Death Kit* to her.) All of this glamourous mysticism that the Taubeses radiated was threatening to me back then; I had a foolish adolescent-atheist animus toward religion as a subject, not yet understanding its possibilities as a gateway to cultural study, and beyond that, even more questionably (though understandable, given my fragile would-be-writer's ego), I had an aversion to taking courses with charismatic professors—both of which reasons combined to prevent me from studying with Susan Sontag, for which I now kick myself.

Nevertheless, I was a member of both the literary and the cinephile circles, which intersected regularly with Sontag. When I wrote my first long story, "The Coffee Drinker," an autobiographical fiction about an unsuccessful suicide attempt, I was urged by friends to show it to a few professors. I got up the nerve to ask Sontag to read it. She generously agreed, in spite of the fact that I was not her student. We met in her office in Philosophy Hall to discuss it. She conveyed, as she often did then, a hearty self-confidence and brio. She seemed too big, too tall for her chair, her arms and legs dangling superfluously. I could tell right away that she hadn't liked the story. How could she? It was in a realist mode, for starters, and heavily psychological—no doubt Dostoyevskian-inflected psychological, since at the time I was reading Dostoyevsky, Dostoyevsky, and more Dostoyevsky. She spared me those positive compliments writing teachers sometimes dispense first before getting to the criticism. She told me I had put in too many details that were not essential, and by way of explaining, said that when she herself was writing a story about a character that was based on her friend Irene (whom I later came to know as the playwright Maria Irene Fornes), she put in that the woman loved to cook spaghetti because Irene loved to cook spaghetti, et cetera. The lesson was that one must never forget fiction and life are different, and that, above all, form must be attended to in making literature. It was just the kind of advice I have often given my writing students, and in its way, it was astute. But of course she had failed to see that flame of genius in me as I had hoped, as the critic Belinsky had seen in Dostoyevesky. I knew she was receptive to youthful literary talent, and had even, in an egalitarian spirit, invited a few of her favorite students to join her own writing group, which met downtown.

In retrospect, I can see that the students she did invite were all engaged in experimental prose, some variation of Nabokov/Beckett/ Burroughs/ Robbe-Grillet that Sontag then saw as the only legitimate fictional path, whereas I was doggedly trying to imbibe the lessons of writers such as Dostoyevsky, Fielding, Kleist, Stendhal, Svevo, and Tolstoy. I am also not sure, in retrospect, that she did such a favor for those undergraduate writers, friends of mine, by promoting them so spectacularly into her own adult literary circle, since they all came down with writer's block.

🔲 Around the same time I had showed her my story, I starting running a film series at Columbia. I programmed obscure foreign art films I wanted to see, as well as classics of Hollywood auteur cinema, and Susan Sontag supported the series by coming regularly. I remember her bringing her barely teenage son, David, to one of the showings, Sam Fuller's *Run of the Arrow*, I believe it was; he looking wispy and gamin-Parisian in his jean jacket, like Jean-Pierre Leaud in *The 400 Blows*.

I would also run into her on the Broadway-104 bus, both of us on our way from campus to a screening at Dan Talbot's New Yorker Theatre, then a mecca for film buffs. She was writing often on movies then, for periodicals such as the *Nation*, *Commentary*, and *Moviegoer*. I was also writing for *Moviegoer* and for the *Supplement* (*Columbia Spectator*), where I reviewed the first New York Film Festival. We would chat about films, belonging to that international brigade of cinephiles whose conversation consists largely of titles and proper nouns, smirks, and grunts— a brittle kind of conversation, steering clear of intimacy, but satisfying in its limited way. On one bus ride she filled me with envy by boasting that she had a permanent free pass to the New Yorker Theatre; it seemed to me as a raw youth the pinnacle of "making it." Decades later, after her death, I learned from Dan and Toby Talbot, who ran the New Yorker, that it was Sontag who came to them and requested an open-ended free pass. They had never issued one but scratched their heads and improvised a reasonable facsimile for her. That request spoke to her already-crystallized sense of the privileges owed her as an emerging public intellectual.

🔲 Another Sontag memory from my youth: a year or two after I had graduated, I went down to the Whitehall Street draft board to demonstrate against the war. It was, as it turned out, one of the more legendary demos, and it started at some preposterous hour like six in the morning. When I got down to the tip of Manhattan, the Whitehall-South Street ferry station, the first person I ran into in the crowd was Susan Sontag. We chatted, she looking around for someone more interesting to spot, and then said with a great girlish squeal, "Oh, there's Benjamin Spock! Doctor Spock!" I turned around, and sure enough, the giraffe-tall, best-selling pediatrician and now antiwar activist was shaking hands with a demonstrator. Sontag beamed with a bobbysoxer's delight. I saw then that celebrities are often star-struck themselves. I liked her very much at that moment. Her girlish enthusiasm was certainly preferable to her other mode, impatient disdain: enthusiasm was her strong suit, her most attractive quality. She went over to Spock and introduced herself, and pretty soon she and the other star demonstrators, including Grace Paley and Dave Dellinger of the War Resisters' League, were cordoned off so that they could be arrested together and peaceably ushered into the waiting paddy wagons, while the rest of us were consigned to march in a circle, chanting "Ho, Ho, Ho Chi Minh" slogans, not even worth getting arrested.

That girlish enthusiasm for father-figures could be quite endearing. For instance, at the first MOMA season of Ozu films, when he was still a secret shared by the cognoscenti, I was sitting in the back of the auditorium with my wife, and we had just seen *Late Spring*, one of the Japanese director's supreme masterpieces, which ends with the old professor left alone at his daughter's marriage. Wiping our eyes as the lights went on, we saw Susan Sontag in the front, wiping *her* eyes. It was a moment uniting us in reverence for the most refined artistry as well as the most common familial emotion, her tears betraying the closet humanist in her, and I nodded to Sontag—but she quickly made it clear that she did not want conversation as she left the hall.

▣ Shortly after I graduated from Columbia, when I had just turned twenty-one, I learned that Alberto Moravia would be speaking at the 92nd Street Y. I was a big fan of Moravia, whose deft, disenchanted shadings of psychological realism in novels, novellas, and short stories delighted me. I made a point of getting tickets well in advance; I would not have missed it for anything. Susan Sontag would be introducing him, an added bonus.

Sontag came onstage and gave an introduction I can only describe as . . . lukewarm. She listed the titles of some of his books, maybe a few of his awards, but withheld the compliments. Then Moravia spoke, for about an hour: his English was excellent, I had no trouble understanding him, but what he said unnerved and disheartened me. He argued that nothing counted in literature except genius and experimental innovation. In the twentieth century, Joyce mattered, Proust mattered, and not much else would survive. Since he himself was not what might be called an "experimental writer," the implication was that he wouldn't be remembered, either; it was as if he were committing literary hari-kari onstage. Here was the author whom I admired as much as anyone alive, telling me he didn't amount to much; and, by extension, my own resistance to the avant-garde's siren song and my allegiance to realism was a waste of time.

Later—I don't remember how—I managed to wrangle a pass into the Green Room, so that

I could be closer to my idol Moravia. He was swamped by well-wishers and fans, and in the meantime I went up to Sontag, whom I knew, after all, however tangentially. "Susan," I said, "You didn't sound so enthusiastic about Moravia in your introduction."

"No, I'm not," she said emphatically, "he's a second-rater. I MUCH PREFER LANDOLFI!" Since she spoke, as was her wont, in a fairly loud voice, and Moravia stood only twenty feet away across the room, I immediately feared he might hear her. Sontag did not seem concerned about that in the least, however. What mattered to her, apparently, was to be seen betting on the right horse, aesthetically speaking. She may have agreed to introduce Moravia at the Y because of her stature as a literary internationalist, but she did not want anyone to get the wrong idea that she actually respected him. We chatted about Tomasso Landolfi for a minute or two: I had read his collection, *Gogol's Wife*, which seemed high-spirited and obviously more experimental than Moravia's work, though to my mind less pungent. I now realized how Moravia's self-undermining speech neatly coincided with Sontag's own preference for avant-garde writing over his brand of psychological realism. Her recently published novel, *The Benefactor*, was in form certainly more Landolfian than Moravian.

Seeing Moravia start to leave out of the corner of my eye, I pulled myself away and approached him. "Signor Moravia," I blurted out, "I am a huge fan of your work, I'm a young writer and I would love to get a chance to speak to you for a few minutes while you are in New York."

Moravia, who had an eagle-like profile, a sharp beak and a prominent bald head, a dandified camel cashmere coat slung over his shoulders, looked me over imperiously and demanded, with his head pulled far away from me: "Speak."

I realized I was being put in my place, or given the opposite of an opportunity to speak. Meanwhile an Italian woman in a fur coat was calling "Alberto, Alberto, the taxi is waiting!" and I said: "Well, you have to go." He turned on his heels and left.

That a famous writer should be abrupt with an importuning fan was not surprising; I had not really expected anything else, and regretted having accosted my idol in this possibly annoying way. What *was* shocking and educational was the combination of Sontag's ungraciousness, Moravia's bitter self-disparagement, and his frostiness afterwards. So *this* was the literary life to which I aspired!

In fact, Moravia was prophetic that night: his literary stock declined from about that point onward, and for at least a decade after his death he was almost forgotten. Then a slow revisionist correction (brought about partly through the insistent efforts of the respected translator William Weaver) began to take place, and now his works are once again being reissued, and he is again regarded as an important modern Italian writer.

Politics and Personae

When Susan Sontag burst on the scene in the early 1960s, she encountered a peculiarly stalemated political context amongst New York intellectuals (the vast majority of whom were allied with the Left). Decades of internecine warfare, from the 1930s to the late 1950s, between the Trotskyites and the Stalinists, the utopian social democrats and the pragmatic ex–New Dealers, had led to a kind of political exhaustion. The veteran ex-debaters of the CCNY cafeteria, such as Irving Howe, Irving Kristol, Norman Podhoretz, and Nathan Glazer, had taken their arguments into the pages of *Partisan Review* and *Commentary* and the *New Leader* and *Dissent.* Every essayist of note had put his or her two cents in on Alger Hiss and Whitaker Chambers, the Rosenberg case, the Eichmann trial, and the Cold War, while the ghosts of past progressive causes, Sacco and Vanzetti, the Scottsboro Boys, et cetera, still hung in the air. The querulous staleness affecting this milieu was wittily captured by Lionel Abel's memoir, *The Intellectual Follies*, in the chapter recalling a group of representative New York intellectuals (Dwight Macdonald, Paul Goodman, Mary McCarthy, Meyer Schapiro, William Phillips, Harold Rosenberg, Hannah Arendt, Norman Podhoretz, Eric Bentley) who met one evening in 1958 to determine what their response should be to the Soviet government's refusal to allow Boris Pasternak to travel to Sweden and collect his Nobel Prize in literature. On the one hand, their membership in the Republic of Letters argued that they must take a firm stand for Pasternak's freedom of speech and against the Soviet government's highhandedness; on the other hand, any condemnation of Soviet Russia would be seen as giving aid to the Cold War, and to the anticommunist, blacklisting Right. Political differences were sharpened by personal animosities: "In fact, Dwight did have something against Paul, an article in *Dissent* in which Goodman had described Dwight as a man who thought with his typewriter. To complicate matters, Dwight that evening was also involved in a running battle with Harold Rosenberg, who had called him a Philistine in *Dissent* for his views on contemporary art," wrote Abel. In the end, the two factions could not agree, and no statement was issued one way or the other.

Sontag for the most part ignored all that past history of factionalism and bad blood. She was clever enough to realize that it no longer "played," and sufficiently youthful herself to feel it held little attraction or relevance for the young, and she threw in politically with the New Left, as opposed to the Old. That is, her politics emphasized anti-imperialism and sexual freedom, while de-emphasizing the working class or any Marxist economic analysis. As a young graduate student married to Philip Rieff, she and he lived for a year with Herbert Marcuse, and Sontag seems to have been much affected by Marcuse's "repressive-tolerance" argument, itself an outgrowth of the Frankfurt School of cultural criticism (Adorno, Horkheimer, et cetera), which located the source of the problem—a docile conformist populace—in capitalist consumerism and mass culture, rather than in the factory and the picket line. She was also intrigued by Norman O. Brown's advocacy of "polymorphous sexuality" in *Life Against Death*, which derived in part from Wilhelm Reich's ideas about the body as the contested site of state control, molded by patriarchal family structure and sexual puritanism. In her 1961 essay "Piety Without Content," she listed with approbation Freudian "dissidents such as Wilhelm Reich, Herbert Marcuse (*Eros and Civilization*) and Norman Brown (*Life Against Death*)" (AI, 255).

If she was a true revolutionary anywhere, then, it was in the area of sexuality. From the start she was looking for a radical politics that would merge justice with sexiness and sensuality, for a revolution that would "swing." She found something like her paradise of sensual bright colors in Cuba, where she stayed for three happy months in 1960, charmed by the revolutionaries' "populist manners" and their "informal, impulsive, easily intimate, and manic, even marathon talkers" (TTH, 31), and continued to be involved in the Fair Play for Cuba committee. But she was put off by the drab grey puritanism of North Vietnam. *Trip to Hanoi*, which was published initially in that revolutionarily pivotal year, 1968, in *Esquire* and as a small, 91-page paperback, is a remarkable piece of writing. Especially the first 39 pages, where she (or the I-character, "Susan Sontag") comes across as more appealingly uncertain and honest than perhaps anywhere else in her work. In extremely long, sweeping paragraphs, many taken directly from her trip diaries—sharply written, articulate and candid—Sontag confesses to her bafflement, frustration, uneasiness, and estrangement. She doubts "that my account of such a trip could add anything new to the already eloquent opposition to the war" (TTH, 3); she finds that "the first days of my stay were profoundly discouraging" (TTH, 4), and rather touchingly confesses, in an admission of her celebrity worship, "The first experience of being there absurdly resembled meeting a favorite movie star, one who for years has played a role in one's fantasy life, and finding the actual person so much smaller, less vivid, less erotically charged, and mainly different" (TTH, 8). Essentially, she and her group were being led around by the nose and fed propaganda, though, being so passionate a partisan of the North Vietnamese, she could not quite admit that to herself, could only register the puzzling flatness of the experience, compared to the rich assortment of images and speculations she had brought to that war-torn country. She drew closer to her traveling companions, with whom she discussed San Francisco rock bands, and admitted guiltily that she missed a psychological or ironical dimension in the moralistic briefings and self-presentations of her tour guides. In other words, she was not succeeding in perceiving her North

Vietnamese hosts as rounded human beings, and wondered if it were her fault or their fault.

A little less than halfway into the essay, at about page 40, she does a sudden 180-degree reversal and decides that it is all her fault, the NLF is exemplary and she is a spoiled Westerner. She cons herself into denying the evidence of her senses: "But the subjective interludes, which I have partly transcribed, convey something else— the callousness and stinginess of my response" (TTH, 40). This is not searching self-scrutiny so much as rote self-criticism, Maoist style. She discovers the propagandist language to be "richer than I'd thought. . . . Much of the discourse we would dismiss as propagandistic or manipulative possesses a depth for the Vietnamese to which we are insensitive" (TTH, 46). She opines, Maoist-fashion, that those hundreds of thousands of city-dwellers now dispersed to the countryside "find themselves thriving psychically on physical austerity and the community-mindedness of rural life" (TTH, 63). Fighting down her own skeptical stirrings, she writes:

> If some of what I've written evokes the very cliché of the Western left-wing intellectual idealizing an agrarian revolution that I was so set on not being, I must reply that a cliché is a cliché,

truth is truth, and direct experience is—well—something one repudiates at one's peril. In the end I can only avow that, armed with these very self-suspicions, I found, through direct experience, North Vietnam to be a place which, in many respects, *deserves* to be idealized. (TTH, 72)

Thus she admits, in black and white, that she is idealizing the North Vietnamese, but asserts that they deserve nothing less.

Swallowing further doubts about the dictatorial apparatus of the communist Party, her sentimental apotheosis is reached when she sees a commissar welling up with tears, which convinces her that

the government loves the people. I remember the poignant, intimate tones in Pham Van Dong's voice as he described the sufferings the Vietnamese have endured in the last quarter of a century and their heroism, decency, and essential innocence. Seeing for the first time in my life a prime minister praising the moral character of his country's people with tears in his eyes has modified my ideas about the conceivable relations between ruler and ruled, and given me a more complex reaction to what I would ordinarily dismiss as mere propaganda. (TTH, 76)

This is very foolish, but it's also brave of her to have gone so far out on a limb for what she believed at the moment. It shows the depth of Sontag's *need* to believe, or rather, using her preferred word, to feel "enthusiasm." Part of what makes her essayist voice so exciting and audacious—but also untrustworthy at times—is the violence she does to her own sense of caution and skepticism, by coercing herself to push ideas and feelings to their most extreme formulation. *Trip to Hanoi* was included in her second essay collection, *Styles of Radical Will*, a title that attested to that self-punishing drive to be "radical" at all costs. (For the New Left, as for Sontag, the term "radical"—a tautological buzz-word never exactly defined, but left as an ever-shifting ideal, to be clung to all the more—came to represent an emotional rallying-point, replacing the economic analysis and class warfare of the Old Left, in politics and culture as well.)

One of the wackiest passages in *Trip to Hanoi* involves her favorable comparison of Vietnamese suffering to Jewish suffering:

> More than once, observing the incredible matter-of-factness of the Vietnamese, I thought of the Jews' more wasteful and more brilliant style of meeting their historical destiny of chronic

suffering and struggle. One advantage of the Vietnamese over the Jews as a martyr people, perhaps, is simply that of any culture dominated by the peasant type over a culture that has crystallized into an urban bourgeoisie. Unlike the Jews, the Vietnamese belong to a culture whose various psychic types have not yet reached a high degree of articulation (forcing them to reflect upon *each other*). It is also the advantage of having a history, albeit mainly of cruel persecution, that is anchored to a land with which people identify themselves, rather than simply (and, therefore, complicatedly) to an "identity."

The Jews' manner of experiencing their suffering was direct, emotional, persuasive. It ran the gamut from stark declamation to ironic self-mockery. It attempted to engage the sympathy of others. At the same time, it projected a despair over the difficulties of engaging others. The source of the Jewish stubbornness, of their miraculous talent for survival, is their surrender to a complex kind of pessimism. Perhaps something like the Jewish (and also "Western") style of overt expressive suffering was what I unconsciously expected to find when I came to Vietnam. That would explain why at first I took for opaqueness and naiveté the quite different way the Vietnamese have of experiencing a comparably tragic history. (TTH, 56–57)

If you can look past the fancy footwork of this tricky, disturbing passage, you see Sontag still trying to apologize, or account for, her originally unenthusiastic response to the Vietnamese. They weren't Jewish enough. At the same time, you can intuit her desire to escape her own Jewishness and learn a more ancient, stoical-peasant, less hysterically self-reflective response to suffering. It is noteworthy that Sontag never identifies herself as a Jew in this passage, though she would have assumed most readers knew that fact about her. She did state that she was Jewish many times in her writing, always somewhat ambivalently, taking pains to assert that she came from generations of "secular" Jews—not a whiff of the old shtetl theology attached. One could say a good deal more about Sontag's relationship to Judaism, a subject she both shied away from and kept touching on tangentially, like a moth to the flame. In *On Photography* she characterized Diane Arbus, for instance, as in "revolt against the Jews' hyper-developed moral sensibility," and spoke of "the ambivalence toward success which afflicted the children of the Jewish upper middle classes in the 1960s" (OP, 44–45).

Sontag herself seems in many ways a paradigm of the Jewish middle-class radical tradition, embodying that "critical spirit" which she herself identified as a specifically Jewish trait. I think she took some pride in being Jewish, and happily assumed her place, after migrating to the East Coast, in the circle of New York Jewish intellectuals. But I also think she equated "grace" and "transparency," two of her desiderata, with not being Jewish, and it is clear from the above passage that optimism belonged in that non-Jewish category as well. At this time in her life Sontag still had optimism, hoping there existed a state of grace, probably somewhere in the Third World, for people of color, if not for her. Jews were not only relentless interpreters, psychologizers, and pessimists, they were also part of the white race which she had excoriated in "What's Happening in America (1966)," two years before *Trip to Hanoi*, by writing:

> The white race is the cancer of human history: it is the white race and it alone—its ideologies and inventions—which eradicates autonomous civilizations wherever it spreads, which has upset the ecological balance of the planet, which now threatens the very existence of life itself. What the Mongol hordes threaten is far less frighten-

ing than the damage that Western "Faustian" man, with his idealism, his magnificent art, his sense of intellectual adventure, his world-devouring energies for conquest, has already done, and further threatens to do. (SRW, 203)

This is high-sixties rhetoric, in the same vein and at roughly the same time as Godard calling for the destruction of the opera houses. Sontag, journeying to Hanoi, would learn the downside of daily life without the cultural accoutrements of Western "Faustian" man. But she would suppress her reservations and play by the junket's rules, writing a book-length essay that would praise her hosts and, she hoped, prove modestly useful to the antiwar movement.

In a strong essay written sixteen years later, "Questions of Travel," Sontag frankly and shrewdly detonates the naive position of her earlier Hanoi text:

The sort of person who writes a book about travel to a communist country is, more often than not, the sort who gets invited. . . . Led from museums to model kindergartens to the birthplace of the country's most famous composer or poet, welcomed and given tea and phony statistics by dignitaries in factories and commutes, shepherded from oversized meal to oversized meal, with time off for shopping sprees in stores reserved for foreigners, the travelers will complete the tightly scheduled trip having talked with hardly anyone except each other and the only natives they spend time with, upon whom they will base many a generalization: the inveterately amiable guides to the delegation. . . . In the Grand Tour offered to visitors to communist countries, travel is designed to make sure the visitor does not encounter anything contaminating. (WSF, 281–83)

It could be argued, I suppose, that such statements merely reflect another kind of oversimplified political bias, one several degrees to the right of her former position. I don't think so; I think she is writing here from rock-bottom, experientially disillusioned reality. In that same essay, she summarizes the options: "The generalizing of travel results in a new genre of travel writing: the literature of disappointment, which from now on will rival the literature of idealization" (WSF, 277). Seen in that light, *Trip to Hanoi* represents a confusing if energetic mix of both options.

Some of Sontag's most politically doctrinaire statements occurred in writings she chose not to include in her later essay collections. They demonstrated her need at the time to come off as a radical, and her chameleonic adaptation of political rhetoric. For instance, in her long introduction to the 1970 book, *The Art of Revolution: 96 Posters from Cuba*, the first section is a beautifully executed synthesis of the history of poster art, showing her capacity to research, assimilate, and summarize masses of material, while the last two sections turn into a tendentious rant with stereotypical language ("satraps"), ending in a sort of verbal raised fist: "Viva Fidel!" She writes: "The Cuban use of political posters recalls Mayakovsky's vision in the early 1920s, before Stalinist oppression crushed the independent revolutionary artists and scrapped the communist-humanist goals of creating better types of human beings" (AR, 7). Ah yes, the New Man, the very mention of which makes me nostalgic, recalling all that effort among us leftists to distance the "communist-humanist" side of the early Marx from the later, authoritarian Marx who paved the way for Stalinism. With a severe tone, Sontag goes on to warn buyers of the Cuban poster book that they are not getting the pure revolutionary deal, but

a tacit betrayal of that use. For, whatever their ultimate artistic and political value, the Cuban posters arise from the genuine situation of a people undergoing profound revolutionary change. Those who produce this book, those like most people who will buy it and read it, live in counter-revolutionary societies, societies with a flair for ripping any object out of context and turning it into an object of consumption. Thus it would not be altogether just to praise those who have made this book. Especially Cuba's foreign friends, as well as those who merely lean toward a favorable review of the Cuban Revolution, should not feel altogether comfortable as they look through it. (AR, 16)

This is Sontag at her most off-putting and Robespierrean. So what if I get pleasure from looking at these poster reproductions? Doesn't it at least give me an insight into one facet of Cuban revolutionary expression? But no, she wants to infect the browser with guilt, the way she later will do with admirers of photography—to accuse us of being superficial tourists.

Did she really believe that when she wrote it? Obviously she chose not to reprint certain polemical pieces in her essay collections because she no longer held those positions, but the other reason is that those pieces have a dutiful, cranked-out quality; they're not her best writing by any means. She was being the good soldier and doing her part for the revolution, while trying on a rhetoric. Something similar occurs with "The Third World of Women," which she wrote in 1972 during the brief season when she tried to be a card-carrying feminist. Here is her list of recommended tactics, reasonable and cockeyed jumbled together:

> Women should lobby, demonstrate, march. They should take karate lessons. They should whistle at men in the streets, raid beauty parlors, picket toy manufacturers who produce sexist toys, convert in sizeable numbers to militant lesbianism, operate their own free psychiatric and abortion clinics, provide feminist divorce counselling, establish make-up withdrawal centers, adopt their mothers' family names as their last names, deface billboard advertising that insults women, disrupt public events by singing in honor of the docile wives of male celebrities and politicians, collect pledges to renounce alimony and giggling, bring law suits for defamation against mass-circulation "women's magazines," conduct telephone harassment campaigns against male psychiatrists who have sexual relations with their women patients, organize beauty contests for

men, put up feminist candidates for all public offices. (TWW, 196–97)

Renounce giggling—I like that. Sontag probably never was much of a giggler, so for her it wouldn't entail considerable sacrifice. The list ends with: "I do not exclude the utility of real guerrilla violence as well."

Her main political energies in this piece, as was often the case, went toward arguing the need to stay radical: "The important difference is not between short-term and long-term objectives but between objectives which are reformist (or liberal) and those which are radical." Suffrage and the legalization of abortion are reformist demands, "and as such suspect." In her politics as in her aesthetics (the avant-garde artist should never compromise with humanist-realism), Sontag disdained all meliorist compromise. If I don't happen to share that attitude, it may be a question of temperament: it doesn't mean I'm right or she's wrong. We do need people who will articulate the radical position. But Sontag's radical feminism strikes me as hasty and poorly thought-out, like a latecomer trying to catch up by including everything.

The end of the Vietnam War marked the cessation of Sontag's most passionate and deeply felt political commitment. So long as she was part of the antiwar movement, she was also in step with youth. In her questionnaire response, "What's Happening in America (1966)," she said:

> I do find much promise in the activities of young people. About the only promise one can find anywhere in this country today is in the way some young people are carrying on, making a fuss. I include both their renewed interest in politics (as protest and as community action, rather than as theory) and the way they dance, dress, wear their hair, riot, make love. I also include the homage they pay to Oriental thought and rituals. And I include, not least of all, their interest in taking drugs—despite the unspeakable vulgarization of the project by Leary and others. (SRW, 199)

When I, at age twenty-three, came across her saying this in the *Partisan Review*, I winced, resenting what sounded like Sontag pandering to youth. Here was someone older and worldlier approving of my generation for looking good, if lacking the smarts for political theory. I, too, wore bell bottoms and red-flowered shirts and took drugs and wanted to make as much love as possible, but I also wanted most of all to be intelligent, like Susan Sontag. It bothered me when older people at anti-war rallies flattered the young as the world's last great hope; I knew we were screwed-up and hadn't a clue what we were doing.

In any case, Sontag eventually came to that conclusion, too, that young people were not the answer. She was drifting further and further into high culture, becoming enamored of opera and ballet, while the youth of the seventies and eighties had increasingly attached themselves to television, MTV, and pop culture, at the same time severing their ties with political idealism. Her early references to pop culture waned—maybe she felt that pop and youth culture no longer needed her defending; they were ubiquitous—and she became the high priestess of seriousness, defending Wagner and Sebald. Craig Seligman and Camille Paglia took her to task for not writing about Prince, but I thought she had put in her time in pop culture criticism; she had every right to move on. We didn't need Sontag to write about Prince; we needed her for other things. In any case, her political turn to the right—or what was seen as such—had a larger role in undercutting her credibility with youth than her lapsed interest in rock music.

Bêtes Noires

◫ From the start, Sontag had certain pet dislikes, the principal ones being "realism," "naturalism," "psychology," and "humanism," almost always placed in quotes, to show that they were charlatans unaware of their fallacy and inauthenticity. She also spoke out, at times, against consumerist materialism and the personal (meaning, the vulgar error of writing about oneself), although these targets were not lifelong bêtes noires, and therefore did not require quotation marks. Since critics are often people with large stores of anger and indignation, it was valid for Sontag to put forth consistent dislikes; they implied a set of standards. The problem occurred when she would encounter one of these shibboleths in her essay, and then all play of doubt would cease while she gave that concept a good smack on the head. (In this she resembled Gore Vidal, another graceful, far-ranging essayist inclined to boilerplate inveighing against key enemy concepts). Structurally, it was as if she were maneuvering the essay until it could square off against one of these familiar patsies, these exhausted traditional values skewered by current intellectual taste, and then she could coast on certainty for a sentence or paragraph. The downsides to this approach were repetition, unsurprise, and a sort of willed narrowness: she could only dismiss these ideals by denying whatever validity they still possessed.

For instance, humanism. In "On Style," she would speak of art's need "to fend off tired ideologies like humanism or socialist realism which would put art in the service of some moral or social idea" (AI, 30–31). To me, humanism is a noble, evergreen concept; to her it is old-hat, ready to be lumped with such artistic atrocities as socialist realism. The intellectual roots of antihumanism can be traced from Nietzsche and Sorel though Heidegger to Sartre and Fanon, who saw it as a universalist banner of colonial conquest. In aesthetic terms, humanism had become, so the claim went, too easy, a yawn: the pieties of the Family of Man photography show. But Sontag came to realize, as the twentieth century wore on, that there are worse things in life than humanism. Many writers she praised in her final years, such as Victor Serge, were nothing if not humanistic, and *Regarding the Pain of Others* was in essence a humanist reassessment of the scornful tone of *On Photography*. In the end, she had had to adjust her scorn.

Regarding "realism," her own failed experimental fiction brought her around to a more naturalistic narrative style in her last two novels,

The Volcano Lover and *In America*. It must have been humbling to discover the sturdy strengths of that tradition. Still, she continued to be a card-carrying antirealist, and to inveigh against its presumptuous reinforcement of the status quo. "In the modern era, the call for a return to realism in the arts often goes hand in hand with the strengthening of cynical realism in political discourse" (ATST, 219), she said in her 2004 Nadine Gordimer Lecture, a few months before she died.

Sontag's attitude toward psychology was more perplexing, ranging from outright hostility to accommodation. On the one hand, nothing could be more in line with avant-garde thinking of the sixties and seventies than a dismissal of psychology. The narrative arts of fiction and film were bored with establishing behavioral causality in characters, and fascinated with what Gide called the *acte gratuite*, the freedom of having characters act without recourse to explanation via environmental influences. Godard's heroes are never seen with parents;* they spring fully formed—

---

* In her essay on *Vivre Sa Vie*, Sontag praises Godard thus: "That freedom has no psychological interior—that the soul is something to be found not upon but after stripping away the 'inside' of a person—is the radical spiritual doctrine which *Vivre Sa Vie* illustrates" (AI, 205).

the same for Beckett's, Robbe-Grillet's, and Sarraute's protagonists. In speaking approvingly of *nouveau roman* writers Michel Butor, Alain Robbe-Grillet, Claude Simon, and Nathalie Sarraute, Sontag writes: "all they abjure is summed up in the notion of 'psychology'" (AI, 104). She quotes Sarraute: "The word 'psychology' is one that no present-day writer can hear spoken with regard to himself without averting his gaze and blushing" (AI, 106). Sontag herself explains, in her essay on Godard, why psychology had to be evicted from the new narrative:

> And of necessity, this present tense must appear as a somewhat behaviorist, external, anti-psychological view of the human situation. For psychological understanding depends on holding in mind simultaneously the dimensions of a past, present, and future. To see someone psychologically is to lay out temporal coordinates in which he is situated. An art which aims at the present tense cannot aspire to this kind of "depth" or innerness in the portrayal of human beings. The lesson is already clear from the work of Stein and Beckett; Godard demonstrates it for film. (SRW, 180)

Sontag also characterized psychoanalytic theory as "a cipher. . . an immense mobile mass in which almost anything can be found" (AI, 108). She regarded most psychological explanation in criticism as tacky. No one would deny that in postwar Freudian America there was a good deal of spurious psychologizing that translated scepters into phallic symbols and read Antigone's principled opposition to Creon as displaced Oedipal attraction. But Sontag also disliked psychological interpretation because it emphasized content over style, and introspection over transparency, grace.

In her essay on Pavese, she wrote of "the insatiable modern preoccupation with psychology, the latest and most powerful legacy of the Christian tradition of introspection, opened up by Paul and Augustine, which equates the discovery of the self with the discovery of the suffering self" (AI, 42). She seemed intent on disentangling the (suspect, Pauline) roots of psychology and Christianity in order to restore a healthier outlook. She wrote approvingly: "Barthes is constantly making an argument against depth, against the idea that the most real is latent, submerged" (WSF, 81). Decades later, she would come to insist on depth as a cultural value, a mark of evolved civilizations,* but in the sixties she was still taking the Wildean aesthete position that the surface was all that mattered. "Interpretation," which looked below the surface, was therefore the enemy. Since Freud's first major breakthrough was entitled *The Interpretation of Dreams*, and since he extended hermeneutics from dreams to telltale tics, wit-play, and eventually all human behavior, Sontag's impatient disgust with psychology might be interpreted (if one were given to interpretation) as displaced rebellion against her older ex-husband, Philip Rieff, who after all wrote one of the most intelligent studies ever of the founding father, *Freud: The Mind of a Moralist*, and even edited Freud's papers.

Sontag was rumored to have had a rather large hand in helping Rieff write his beautiful tribute to Freud. Rieff says in the acknowledgments to the first edition, "My wife, Susan Rieff, devoted herself unstintingly to this book." Clearly it was

---

* In her 1987 essay on Italian photography, she wrote: "The depth possessed by these images of an older Italy is not just the depth of the past. It is the depth of a whole culture, a culture of incomparable dignity and flavor and bulk, that has been thinned out, effaced, confiscated. To be replaced by a culture in which the notion of depth is meaningless" (WSF, 222).

a project that engaged them both, which meant that Sontag would have had to immerse herself in Freud's oeuvre. For the most part, after leaving Rieff she would stay clear of Freud in her writing. Here, though, in her essay "Psychoanalysis and Norman O. Brown's *Life Against Death*," she draws the line between adjustment and revolt:

> But the disenchantment of American intellectuals with psychoanalytic ideas, as with the earlier disenchantment with Marxist ideas (a parallel case), is premature. Marxism is not Stalinism or the suppression of the Hungarian revolution; psychoanalysis is not the Park Avenue analyst or the suburban matron discussing her child's Oedipus complex. . . . This is the importance of Brown's *Life Against Death*, as well as of Marcuse's *Eros and Civilization*. Brown, like Marcuse, pursues Freud's ideas as a general theory of human nature—not as a therapy which returns people to the society which enforces their conflicts. Psychoanalysis is conceived by Brown not as a mode of treatment to smooth away the neurotic edges of discontent, but as a project for the transformation of human culture, and as a new and higher level in human consciousness as a whole. Freud's psychological cat-

egories are thus correctly seen, in the terminology of Marcuse, as political categories. (AI, 258)

It is fascinating to consider this sleight-of-hand by which Sontag rescues Freud by upgrading him from the "psychological" to the "political." Why the category "political" should be seen as so much more profound and valid than the category "psychological" is a question. And would that it were so easy to "smooth away the neurotic edges of discontent"! Apparently, the "discontent" of the individual is small potatoes, especially if that person is bourgeois. I can't help blanching at Sontag's glib dismissal of the "suburban matron," her caricaturing of the woman by age and geography, which puts her beyond the pale of human suffering. Obviously, this Oedipal mother-son pair was an image she very much wanted to distance herself from.

What is curious is that Sontag in fact had a considerable gift for probing psychological insight, as can be seen, for instance, in her biographical essays on Benjamin, Pavese, Goodman, Canetti, and Artaud. For her to disparage psychology was to squander one of her natural talents. She admitted, tellingly, in *Trip to Hanoi*, that the one thing she missed in this land of exemplary communism was "psychology"; the commisars were not given to gossip or probing each other's motives.

In person, Sontag also conveyed a mixed impression regarding psychological awareness. She often struck me as almost prepsychological, seeming blithely unaware that she was even giving offense, much less leaving a trail of insulted, gasping ex-admirers behind. Living in her head much of the time, she sometimes resembled a math nerd who has not been properly socialized. On the other hand, her recently published diaries reveal that she was quite conscious of her effect on others: "One of my strongest and most fully employed emotions: contempt. Contempt for others, contempt for myself." The diaries show a shrewd if intermittent self-awareness. Terry Castle phrases it this way in her *London Review of Books* (November 5, 2007) memoir-piece: Sontag showed, "when she was in a benign and non-threatened mood, a fair amount of ironic self-knowledge." So one can only conclude that she knew what she was doing, but wanted to continue behaving in a manner that suggested she didn't (that is, was psychologically naive) because it gave her more freedom to act the way she wanted, and not to be held psychologically accountable.

Still, Sontag came to see herself more and more as a moralist, both in political and aesthetic matters, and so at a certain point the question becomes: How can one be a moralist without also being a psychologist? (This was precisely the problem Rieff posed in reverse by the title of his book, *Freud: The Mind of the Moralist*). Can these two forces ever be cleanly disentwined in modern consciousness? Sontag gave it a try, but she paid a price by short-changing one side of her intelligence.

▣ Philip Rieff and Susan Sontag both approved of austerity. Rieff advocated an austerity that resembled Freud's sublimation, the evolved adult's renunciation of the pleasure principle, and the refusal to opt for any easy redemption, transcendence, or salvation. His Freud was the stoic Freud whom Lionel Trilling also revered, who had a high sense of duty. Sontag did not follow that path, calling instead for "an erotics of art," but she was never a sloppy sensualist. Art needed to be puritanically rigorous, to go to extremes. So, too, did hedonism: as with Sade, pleasure required polemics and an ascetic, self-sacrificial streak. The sexual gamesmanship in her first novel, *The Benefactor*, or her first film,

Duet for Cannibals, has a joyless cerebral quality, like a chess match that has lost its savor but that one must still play out to the bitter end. It was as if the only plot that could engage her imagination at this point was *La Ronde*.

Even in following the dictates of sexual liberation, she insisted on rigor: she would have her cake (bisexual experimentation, essays on pornography) and eat it too (restraint, discipline, "seriousness"). But all was not austerity: Sontag, still a young woman, was drawn to rock 'n roll, excited by its expressiveness. "I remember once, I guess it was 1956," she told the *New Yorker*'s Joan Acocella,

> I used to go to my classes and go right home,
> because I had a child and a husband, and why
> wouldn't I go home? But this day, for some rea-
> son—maybe I had had a fight with Philip—
> I didn't go home. I went into the movie theatre
> in Harvard Square. The movie that was playing
> was *Rock Around the Clock*. And I sat there, I
> was twenty-three years old, and I thought, My
> God! This is great! This is absolutely fantastic!
> After the movie I walked home very slowly. I
> thought, Do I tell Philip that I've seen this
> movie—this sort of musical about kids, and it

was wonderful, and there were kids dancing in the aisles? And I thought, No, I can't tell him that. (AATS, 446)

Often, in later life, when she spoke of her early marriage she would compare herself to Dorothea Brooke, the heroine of George Eliot's *Middlemarch*,* and Rieff to the loathsome Casaubon—a rather self-flattering comparison, in that she got to be the ardent young woman destined for efficacy and he, the dry stick of a scholar, a disapproving killjoy who oppressed his young wife and would never complete his projected works. (Rieff actually published a fair amount of ambitious thought in his lifetime. Posthumously, he has even developed a cult-like following, his densely written warnings about the undermining of authority and traditional spirituality proving catnip to some, while leading others to regard the message in them as reactionary. In the mid-eighties I went to a lecture by Rieff, just out of curiosity, or

---

* "I remember when I first read *Middlemarch*: I had just turned eighteen, and a third of the way through the book burst into tears because I realized not only that *I* was Dorothea but that, a few months earlier, I had married Mr. Casaubon" (IA, 25). While this passage appears in a novel, there is no doubt that the speaker is Sontag herself. It duplicates remarks she made in countless interviews.

frankly to get a glimpse of Sontag's ex-husband, and he did seem to hold himself with unnatural rigidity: a stern, embittered man, oddly dandyish in Oxonian three-piece suit.)

Once, when I was getting ready to interview her, Sontag began speaking fondly to me—much to my surprise—about her ex-husband. "We had great talks, Philip and I," she recalled. "We would talk together for hours. I remember we went to a party, and afterwards we drove home and sat in the car discussing everyone. Then the sun came up and it was morning and we realized we had been sitting there all night! How I miss that—that mental rapport in a partner." The words brought forth in her a girlish, leafy, generous spirit, quite at odds with her customary dissatisfied manner. I saw at that moment that I had very little notion of her emotional range.

The marriage of Sontag and Rieff looks more and more improbable in retrospect. He abhorred modernism, which he saw as leading to Psychological Man and the triumph of the therapeutic. She saw modernism as a salvation, and emphasized its difficulty, which required rigor and discipline. Sontag used her reaction against Rieff to catapult her into an energetic defense of modernism, sexual freedom, camp. But the farther away she moved in time from that rebellion against the Dorothea-Casaubon marriage, the weaker became her frisky impulse. And she got older.

Apparently, toward the end of their lives, the ex-couple reached something of a rapprochement, or at least a warmer regard for each other. Rieff dedicated his last book, *My Life Among the Deathworks* (2006), to "Susan Sontag, in remembrance." Much might be read into that single word "remembrance." They had in fact grown closer, if only in their disgust at the unbearable lightness of the surrounding culture. Just as Rieff began by focusing on the emancipating program of Freud but in later years insisted on the need for authority, so did Sontag, in her way, come to embrace authority—except for her, it was to be found neither in religion nor the state, but in seriousness, genius, standards, a literary Parnassus reached only by the agon of difficulty—another dying God.

Crisis as Starting-Point

What did Sontag propose as an alternative to psychology? The answer is spirituality, but a spirituality not to be found in religions, but rather in art of an ascetic nature, which will teach us how to focus attention and see clearly again. Though an art which stresses silence, emptiness, and reduction would appear to be puritanical, it is not, she insists: "there is no talented and rigorous asceticism that, whatever its intention, doesn't produce a gain (rather than a loss) in the capacity of pleasure" (SRW, 8).

"The Aesthetics of Silence," written in 1967 and collected in *Styles of Radical Will*, is one of her most intriguing essays because she manages to approve the aesthetic strategies of "impoverishment and reduction" without minimizing the inevitable contradictions they involve. How can art pursue the ineffability of silence without finally lapsing into silence (the suicides of Kleist and Lautreamont being two extreme cases cited)? How much can art experiment with an anti-art posture and still be executed in good faith? What are the limits of irony?

Many of the essays in her first two collections begin with an overall statement of the crisis of modernism at this particular juncture, and then zero in on one cultural figure who embodies that cul-de-sac or promises a way out of it. A crisis has the advantage of being a dramatic, attention-getting device. It allows Sontag to take a step back and put her subject in a larger context. For instance, there is the crisis of too much historicizing consciousness, analyzed in the essay on E. M. Cioran; the crisis of awareness of the body as a problem, the desire to free ourselves from the ascetic traditions of Judaism and Christianity while still being attached to their mind-sets, described in her essay on Pavese; and the crisis of language and psychology being exhausted or mistrusted, which leads to the paradoxical solutions of antiexpressive expressiveness described in "The Aesthetics of Silence."

The disadvantage of the crisis motif is that it is prone to exaggerating the eleventh-hourness of everything, and of drawing too-narrow terms in the interests of sharpening the dilemma. Thus, Sontag says, in response to the crisis invoked in "The Aesthetics of Silence," that "the artist ends by choosing between two inherently limiting alternatives, forced to take a position that is either servile or insolent. Either he flatters or appeases his audience, giving them what they already know, or he commits an aggression against his audience, giving them what they don't want" (srw, 15). Surely there are other successful alternatives for artists today than these two, such as art that gives audiences what they may not think initially

they want but which they come to find beautiful (Richard Serra, Jasper Johns, Erich Rohmer)
or which they may initially think conventionally
pleasing though it finishes by not flattering but
stretching them (the stories of Peter Taylor or
William Trevor). Moreover, there is something
bullying in sky-is-falling rhetoric that invites
resistance. Sontag herself shows an awareness
of this danger, when she comments wittily that
"this advocacy of silence tends to be frenetic and
overgeneralizing. It is also frequently apocalyptic
and must endure the indignity of all apocalyptic
thinking: namely, to prophecy the end, to see the
day come, to outlive it, and then to set a new date
for the incineration of consciousness and the
definitive pollution of language and exhaustion
of the possibilities of art-discourse" (SRW, 32).

Sontag did not make the mistake herself of
prophesying the end, but she did sound the alarm
a great deal. Some of the crises she pinpointed
still seem highly germane today; others seem to
have been diffused. Such is the risk most cultural
critics take by concentrating on the topical, and
by approaching it from a "crisis" angle.

Situated chronologically just as the curtain
was about to go up on postmodernism, "The
Aesthetics of Silence" has considerable pre-

science, especially in its analysis of "babble" and the limits of irony. Where it seems dated is in its insistence that this one problem (the exhaustion of language, the agony of consciousness) is the crisis that drives all contemporary art today. She refused to acknowledge the possibility that an artist can come along and not be tormented by these questions, and still make good art. A new writer always has the option to refuse the hair-shirt of the contemporary language-crisis and write to his/her heart's content. If by doing so he or she has evaded the historical quandary posed by Beckett, say, well, too bad. Here is an instance where Sontag's conflation of her descriptive and prescriptive modes arouses my sharpest resistance—partly for defensive reasons, but partly because I don't see that important art necessarily grows out of response to any overview of aesthetic-historical crisis

Are the Arts Progressive?

▣ In her 1963 (revised 1965) essay, "Nathalie Sarraute and the Novel," Sontag seemed to be endorsing the idea that "art must evolve. . . . Art is the army by which human sensibility advances implacably into the future, with the aid of ever-newer and more formidable techniques" (AI, 100). If, later, she would gag at militaristic metaphors, as a young critic she embraced the militancy of the avant-garde position.

> While music and the plastic arts and poetry painfully dug themselves out of the inadequate dogmas of 19th-century "realism," by a passionate commitment to the idea of progress in art and a hectic quest for new idioms and new materials, the novel has proved unable to assimilate whatever of genuine quality and spiritual ambition has been performed in its name in the 20th century. It has sunk to the level of an art form deeply, if not irrevocably, compromised by philistinism. (AI, 102)

Let us unpack these sentences. "Philistinism" (Sontag's favorite word of dispraise) is not so much a category of evaluation as a stigmatizing label. There is no way to refute a charge of philistinism; one stands hopelessly convicted in advance. Sontag is saying, in effect: "Come on, Anglo-American Novel, don't embarrass me, look at atonal music and abstract expressionism—get with the program!" Now I don't dispute that these innovations were great advances; I love Schoenberg, Mondrian, Pollock, and Coltrane, too, but I fail to be convinced that literature should undergo the same process of abstraction for its own good. Literature may be composed of a fundamentally different material than music and painting, clinging as it does to the debased, meaning-dependent coin of language. Even in the other arts we have seen, since the midsixties, when Sontag made her argument, some paintings return to figuration and some music to tonality without resulting in the mortal setback of either form. A better model for the arts than linear progression might be the eternal return Nietzsche speaks of, a dialectical recycling of certain tendencies, such as realism or abstraction, that spiral helically toward and away from each other in different eras.

That great nineteenth-century critic William Hazlitt wrote an essay entitled "Why the Arts are Not Progressive," in which he argued:

> First, the complaint itself, that the arts do not attain that progressive degree of perfection which might reasonably be expected from them, proceeds on a false notion, for the analogy appealed to in support of the regular

advances of art to higher degrees of excellence, totally fails; it applies to science, not to art. . . . What is mechanical, reducible to rule, or capable of demonstration, is progressive, and admits of gradual improvement: what is not mechanical or definite, but depends on genius, taste, and feeling, very soon becomes stationary, or retrograde, and loses more than it gains by transfusion.[*]

Sontag was aware of problems in claiming the arts were progressive, but she attempted to get around them by substituting the notion of "radical" for "progressive." She wrote in 1966: "Every interesting aesthetic tendency is a species of radicalism. The question each artist must ask is: What is *my* radicalism, the one dictated by *my* gifts and temperament? That doesn't mean all contemporary artists believe that art progresses. A radical position isn't necessarily a forward-looking position" (SRW, 119). Still, she was claiming that taste (of the most forward-looking, refined kind—her taste) had reached a point that *demanded* the novel be more in step with the rigors of modern

[*] *The Round Table* (1814), in *Selected Essays of William Hazlitt*, ed. Geoffrey Keynes (Nonesuch, 1970), 603–4.

painting and music. ("It is time that the novel become what it is not, in England and America, with rare and unrelated exceptions: a form of art which people with serious and sophisticated taste in the other arts can take seriously" [AI, 111].)

In retrospect, Sontag overplayed the importance of a Robbe-Grillet or Sarraute. She herself later confessed, to the *New Yorker*'s Joan Acocella: "I thought I *liked* William Burroughs and Nathalie Sarraute and Robbe-Grillet, but I didn't. I actually didn't" (JA, 450). She had coerced herself into believing she did because they fit into her argument; they were useful as weapons in her polemic against realism, psychology, philistinism, et cetera. In her most Cassandra manner, she had stated that the triumph of avant-garde fiction was inevitable: "This surrender of the novel's commitment to facileness, to easy availability and the perpetuation of an easy aesthetic, will undoubtedly give rise to a great many boring and pretentious books; and one may well come to wish the old unself-consciousness back again. But the price must be paid" (AI, 103). Actually, her reservations can be sensed even back then, when she wrote that she preferred the polemical essays by the *nouveau roman* authors to their novels because "they propose standards that are ampler and more ambitious than anything yet achieved by any writer. (Robbe-Grillet, for instance, admits that his novels are inadequate illustrations of the diagnoses and recommendations put forth in his essays.)" (AI, 105).

The diagnoses, recommendations, and standards advocated by Robbe-Grillet and taken up by Sontag would affect her own attempts at novel writing, and not always advantageously. For, among the "boring and pretentious novels" that she predicted would ensue by a laborious following out of this radical program of the future, we must count *The Benefactor* and *Death Kit*, as well as many of the stories in *I, etcetera*. But that is matter for a later discussion.

The Stylistics of Demystification

▣ Part of Sontag's original impact consisted in bringing a European tone into American critical prose. An implacably intellectual, paradoxical, mandarin register, derived from French and German cultural criticism, it had the side effect of downplaying the more familiar, conversational, clubbable, British-American belletristic tone.

While outwardly disdaining content analysis and interpretative probes below the surface,

Sontag was deeply imbued with that Continental mind-set that might be called "demystification": the habit of mind that continually seeks the hidden pattern behind the status quo. From Nietzsche, the pioneering demystifier, exposing asceticism as a contorted will to power; to Marx, analyzing "false consciousness"; to Freud's theory of the unconscious positing that we can never be cognizant of our own desires; to Sartre and the French Existentialists' notion of "bad faith"; to Marcuse's oxymoronic "repressive tolerance"; to Barthes's translation of the "mythologies" beneath advertisements and brands—unmasking hidden motives has been a staple of modern thought. In Sontag's case, it went like this: You *think* you only want to take photographs to commemorate an innocent family outing, a vacation abroad, but in reality you are using the camera like a gun; you are an aggressor, a predator appropriating what does not belong to you. You *think* you are speaking of the need for a full-scale war on this or that illness to heighten awareness of the situation's urgency, but by using martial metaphors you are making the patient into a sitting target, a nonhuman.

Demystification discovers, invariably, some dirty secret that society is reluctant to drag out into the open, rather than some unexpected example of altruistic probity. Philip Rieff, in *Freud: The Mind of the Moralist*, amusingly observes that Freud "could infer a hidden sexual meaning from the apparently quite asexual 'violet' which figured in the dream of a woman acquaintance, on the basis of the 'chance similarity' of 'violets' with the English word 'violate'" (79), but the process never worked in reverse; that is, Freud never deduced the name of a flower from a forbidden sexual urge.

The great efforts of the Frankfurt School theoreticians—Adorno, Horkheimer, Benjamin, Habermas, and Marcuse—to analyze the problems of late capitalism resulted in a method that Adorno called "negative dialectics." In diagnosing political pathology, the negative dialectician adopted a manner of weary unsurprise, positioning himself or herself above the fray. As when looking from a great height all things seem flattened, so anger is deferred to the preoccupation with arriving at the correct overview. An insistently demystifying approach may result in a mood of High Sour, wherein every problem or cultural artifact is analyzed in such a way that any possible avenues of escape are closed off one by one (exposed either as preserving the status quo, as liberal bourgeois privatism, or as self-destructive adventurism) until the world comes to seem a claustrophobic place indeed.

Whenever you come across syntaxes like "A is in reality nothing more than B" or "X merely mirrors the power relations of Y" or "E is a cosmetic version of D" or "betrays its true nature as Q," you know you are deep in demystification. It is a land where all the ball bearings run down a triangular wooden block from higher to lower slopes. Its chemistry is based on reductive processes that put each substance through a retort and show it to be less than originally appeared. The greatest modern text in this genre (and a favorite of Sontag's) is Adorno's *Minima Moralia*, a manual for every technique of undercutting. One is left speechless before the flexibility of Adorno's sentences, which twist each hope into a pretzel before choking it to death. Adorno is like someone who has discovered a magic diminishing eyepiece and applies it everywhere with enthusiasm, however bleak his conclusions may be.

The Frankfurt School thinkers and the French structuralists all had belletristic proclivities. They wished to graft Nietzsche's pungency onto Marx, and to borrow the former's stylistic formats: the mini-essay of two pages or less, the aphorism.

This predilection for disconnected fragments, hit-and-run *pensées*, proved particularly valuable for the left at a time when large philosophic systems became suspect.

The aphorism has a number of dialectical appeals. It is a statement that moves in two directions at once. It raises and resolves a paradox; it leaves behind an afterimage, like an op-art painting the clash of whose two colors produce a third on the retina. The aphorism turns toward poetic condensation, thereby borrowing from poetry the associational leap. Kafka's plausible-gnomic style ("There is hope, only not for me") fascinated Benjamin and Adorno, and their sentences at times seemed modeled on his ability to achieve uncannily disillusioned effects.

There is in Adorno, Benjamin, the early Lukacs, Barthes, and their most prominent American disciple, Sontag, a will to aphorize. The prose aspires constantly to ontological assertion. Each aphorism is a tortured quest to arrive at a succinct truth that will nevertheless bring no relief, hammering the intractable material of modern society into its most compact negative form. Each aphorism promises transcendence, through a surcharge of meaning suggested by compacted language, even as it wittily negates all possibility of release.

The trap the aphoristic manner sometimes falls into is to fix the sentence in a gravely abstracted utterance whose crystalline terseness is more portentous than meaningful; the sentence has had all grosser elements burned off, its intention of declaring wisdom everywhere apparent, amidst a bitterly laconic aftertaste, but the effort of demystification to pull off the mask turns into yet another masquerade.

The Aphoristic Essay

⬚ Though she did not invent the form, Sontag was a master of the aphoristic essay. She also wrote keenly and sensitively about aphoristic technique, understanding it from top to bottom.

> The authority of the renowned first sentences of *Pride and Prejudice* and *Anna Karenina* depends on their floating free from any particular speaker, as if it were the nature of wisdom to be impersonal, oracular, anonymous, overbearing. Neither assertion is actually true. Both seem unchallengeably mature and pertinent as impatient observations about the cruelties of the marriage market and the despair of the naïve wife upon discovering her husband's infidel-

ity. This is a strong hand with which to open a novel, some axiom about human behavior offered preemptively or ironically as an eternal verity. ("It is a truth. . ." "All happy families *are*. . .") Knowingness about human nature, old-style, is always in the present tense. (WSF, 16)

She would seem to be describing here her own approach. Many of her essays consist of webs of passive verbs. (Creative-writing teachers commonly instruct their students to stay away from passive verbs, but Sontag demonstrates how wrong that is, how far you can fly on their wings.) Like a prophetess with closed eyes, seeing deep into the nature of things, she declaims one "is/are/seems" verb-sentence after another: the impersonal, the oracular, the anonymous, the present tense and indeed the overbearing are evident, but so is something else from the start— the wish to be wise. ("I am interested in wisdom," she declared boldly and admirably, in *I, etcetera* [15].) A precocious young writer with ambitions to worldliness, such as F. Scott Fitzgerald, James Baldwin, Mary McCarthy, or Susan Sontag may bluff his/her way into the appearance of wisdom by aphorism, and, with genius, luck, or both, hit the mark.

"Every exquisite linguistic moment (or incisive thought) is a matter of stasis, a potential ending. Aphoristic finalities sap forward momentum, which thrives on more loosely woven sentences," Sontag wrote (WSF, 22). That aphoristic sapping of forward momentum was another reason she excelled at shorter essay forms rather than book-length ruminations.

In her superb, penetrating essay on Barthes's stylistics, she gave many other insights into the aphoristic technique:

> Its brilliance aside, Barthes's work has some of the specific traits of a late moment in culture—one that presumes an endless discourse anterior to itself, that presumes intellectual sophistication: it is work that, strenuously unwilling to be boring or obvious, favors compact assertion, writing that rapidly covers a great deal of ground. Barthes was an inspired, ingenious practitioner of the essay and the anti-essay—he had a resistance to long forms. (WSF, 64–65)

Barthes was Sontag's model, especially in the first three essay collections. And we may assume she is speaking of her own ambitions, too, when she lauds Barthes for gallantly paying the intelligent reader the compliment of not boring anyone with excessive preliminary explanation.

> While exuding straight-ahead energy, his prose constantly reaches for the summative formulation; it is irrepressibly aphoristic. . . . Barthes's strengths as an aphorist suggest a sensibility gifted, before any intervention of theory, for the perception of structure. A method of condensed assertion by means of symmetrically counterposed terms, the aphorism displays the symmetries of situations and ideas—their design, their shape. Like a markedly greater feeling for drawings than for paintings, a talent for aphorism is one of the signs of what could be called the formalist temperament. (WSF, 65)

So aphorism becomes the shield of formalism, one of her main causes. But how lovely, that phrase: "the symmetries of situations and ideas"! Again, Sontag seems to be alerting us to her own X-ray gifts for perception of structure, which are apparent in whatever she is writing about.

She has several more pungent things to say about this subject, which reveal her underlying attraction to the technique: "It is the nature of aphoristic thinking to be always in the state of concluding: a bid to have the final word is inherent in all powerful phrase-making" (WSF, 67). "Drawn to hyperbole, as all aphorists are ..." (WSF, 68). "Of a variety of means Barthes possessed for giving himself something to say—he had an exceptionally fluent, ingenious generalizing power—the most elementary was his aphorist's ability to conjure up a vivacious duality; anything could be split either into itself and its opposite or into two versions of itself; and one term then fielded against the other to yield an unexpected relation" (WSF, 67).

When Sontag stumbled, put her foot in her mouth, it invariably arose from the will to aphorize. Her periodic tin ear lured her into making hyperbolic statements such as "The white race is the cancer of humanity" (which she later regretted, not because it defamed millions of people but because it metaphorized illness) or "Communism is Fascism with a human face." In that same speech on communism, she would declare that readers of *Readers Digest* got more of the truth than those of the *Nation*. At the moment she probably thought she was bravely telling her audience an unpopular truth, but she was in fact closing herself off to nuance and complexity. That is, she was not proposing a "vivacious duality," like Barthes, that splits a meaning into its opposite; she was simply having "the final word."

In general, you could say that Sontag admired certain traits in Barthes—wily affability, amusement rather than 'outrage or indignation, slipping the noose of the doctrinaire—that she herself was unable to appropriate. She knew what that dual-toned, subtly evocative, mellifluous discourse sounded like, and she aspired to it, but again and again she found herself getting on her high horse and moralizing, to her later chagrin. In her *Paris Review* interview she said, hearing herself quoted on war, "That prescriptive voice rather makes me cringe." And in "Thirty Years Later," her retrospective take on *Against Interpretation*, she described herself as having been "a pugnacious aesthete and a barely closeted moralist. . . . What I don't like are those passages in which my pedagogic impulses got in the way of my prose. Those lists, those recommendations! I suppose they are useful, but they annoy me now" (WSF, 270). Granted, she couldn't duplicate Barthes's sangfroid or Benjamin's feline, shape-shifting elusiveness. But it's in the gap between imitating a master and not being able to duplicate the grand manner that one's own originality is discovered, and often what is valued in Sontag is her moral passion, her emotional force, her pedagogic engagement.

The Film Essays

Sontag loved movies, so it is no accident that some of her strongest writing was about them. She did most of these pieces in the sixties, a high point both for cinema and film criticism. Although she never held down a regular perch as a reviewer, and discussed for the most part only directors she admired, I would not hesitate to include her among the best American film critics. One reason her film essays were so good, so knowledgeable, penetrating, thoughtful, and judicious, was that she gave movies more of a free pass, and did not feel compelled to indict them for failing to forfeit realism, psychology, or other impurities. In her essay "Against Interpretation" she wrote:

> Ideally, it is possible to elude the interpreters in another way, by making works of art whose surface is so unified and clean, whose momentum is so rapid, whose address is so direct that the work can be. . . just what it is. Is this possible now? It does happen in films, I believe. This is why cinema is the most alive, the most exciting, the most important of all art forms right now. Perhaps the way one tells how alive a particular art form is, is

by the latitude it gives for making mistakes in it, and still being good. (AI, 11)

She goes on to say, sounding rather like Pauline Kael, that the medium's resistance to the evils of interpretation is in part explainable by "the happy accident that films for such a long time were just movies; in other words, that they were understood to be part of mass, as opposed to high, culture, and were left alone by most people with minds" (AI, 12).

▣ Two of her most original film pieces were on science fiction and on the relationship between theatre and film. "The Imagination of Disaster" is a relaxed, witty performance that moves from a dissection of the typical science fiction film's structure—1) the arrival of the thing; 2) reports of destruction; 3) conferences between scientists and world leaders; 4) further atrocities; 5) final repulse of the monster or invaders—to an analysis of the genre's appeal (we get to experience in substitute form our own death, enjoy the mayhem and the cruel "thrill of watching all those expensive sets come tumbling down"), ending in speculation about possible connections between the genre's naive formulae and the anxieties of the nuclear age. ("Ours is indeed an age of extremity. For we live under continual threat of two equally fearful but seemingly opposed, destinies: unremitting banality and inconceivable terror" [AI, 224].) For the most part, freed from her need to play the priestess of High Taste, she can enjoy herself like a regular moviegoer: "Lines like 'Come quickly, there's a monster in my bathtub,' 'We must do something about this,' 'Wait, Professor. There's someone on the telephone,' 'But that's incredible,' and the old American stand-by, 'I hope it works!' are hilarious in the context of picturesque and deafening holocaust" (AI, 225).

"Theatre and Film," a 1966 essay reprinted in *Styles of Radical Will*, is more dryly written, but nonetheless audaciously original. It shows her ability to question received opinion: in this case, that cinema needed to purge itself of theatrical elements to find its truer, purer nature. Sontag dismantles fifty years of prejudices about the ostensible opposition between the two arts, and in the process takes on such authorities as Erwin Panofsky and Siegfried Kracauer. Panofsky had argued in his celebrated essay, "Style and Medium in the Motion Pictures," that what made something cinematic was a mobile camera exploring space, and that articulate, literate dialogue or voice-over ("even, I am grieved to say, some of the wisecracks of Groucho Marx," he wrote) destroyed the cinematic illusion. Sontag rebuts this narrow position that the sound element in film must always be subordinate to the visual, or that a static camera is perforce uncinematic, with examples from Bresson, Ozu, Godard, Dreyer, Kurosawa, and Cocteau. She easily punctures Kracauer's assertion that the cinema must be committed to "reality," which would make neorealism the only permitted style and movies shot in real-life locations invariably better than those shot in studios. Thus she maneuvers the essay to blast her customary bête noire, the unexamined claims of realism's "authenticity," and to defend the elements of artifice and abstraction in art. In this case, her doctrinaire stance has the salutary effect of expanding possibilities: "But there is no reason to insist on a single model for film" (SRW, 102), she concludes. Sontag's feeling for the theatre, an art form she enjoyed both as spectator and practitioner, enabled her to bring the requisite sensitivity and wisdom to these territorial issues.

Sontag's essay "Spiritual style in the films of Robert Bresson," is a superb summation of that rigorous filmmaker. As with many of her introductions to the American public of some cultural figure, she begins by the rhetorical device of asserting that Bresson is underappreciated but great, and goes on to explain why he is underappreciated by Americans (his art is "reflective," "it invites the use of intelligence" rather than identification with characters), and why it is great. Characteristically, too, she situates her main subject between several other figures—Brecht, Cocteau and Ozu—the better to bring out his uniqueness. Self-effacingly, she surrenders to Bresson, content to describe what the master does, what his films look like—a departure from her more polemically aggressive pieces in *Against Interpretation*. But Bresson is also the hero of that collection, in that he exemplifies the disappearance of content into form.

> Whatever is not necessary, whatever is merely anecdotal or decorative, must be left out. . . . For Bresson, art is the discovery of what is necessary—of that, and nothing more. The power of Bresson's six films lies in the fact that his purity and fastidiousness are not just an assertion about the resources of the cinema, as much of modern painting is mainly a comment in paint about painting. They are at the same time an idea about life, about what Cocteau called "inner style," about the most serious way of being human. (AI, 194–5)

That last sentence (it is also in fact the last sentence of the essay) has that recognizably high-flown if cryptic tone of early Sontag, which both lyrically evokes a meaning just beyond reach and forestalls further argument. Since I also cherish Bresson, I am prepared to grant him any compliment, especially one so handsome, though I am not exactly certain what she means with "an idea about life" or "inner style" or "the most serious way of being human." What I see is that she is trying to reconcile two aesthetics, the formalist (painting is just about paint) and the humanist (art is about life and being human). Usually she has no patience with the second, but since Bresson is such a transcendent artist, she reaches for that hitherto-despised humanist vocabulary as a way of putting the crown on his seriousness.

Sontag's two essays on Jean-Luc Godard show her determination to pin down this key late-modernist innovator as an exemplary standard-bearer for her aesthetic. The first, "Godard's *Vivre Sa Vie*," playfully mimics the film's twelve-chapter structure by its own division into seventeen segments and an appendix. Otherwise, however, Sontag's tone here is anything but playful; it is pedagogic, Calvinist, gnomic, as we glean from the first, warning sentence: "Preface: *Vivre Sa Vie* invites a rather theoretical treatment, because it is—intellectually, aesthetically—extremely complex" (AI, 196). Eat your spinach. She finds in this film so many corroborations of her "against-interpretation" thesis that the fit comes to seem a little too convenient. She says Godard "proves," he doesn't "analyze"; analysis is "interminable," incomplete, therefore the analytical artist doesn't know how to end, therefore is deficient in form. On the other hand, Godard's film "rejects causality. . . . [I]t shows that something happened, not why it happened;" it is "drastically untopical" and uninterested in the sociological aspects of prostitution—it is in short a "demonstration," which "exposes the inexorability of an event," take it or leave it. I find every one of these assertions debatable, and vaguely tautological. It happens because it had to happen? Then why should "causality" undercut "inexorability"? It is impossible for an audience not to intuit, or at least project, some elements of causality onto the poignant, linear narrative of Nana's life and death. Sontag is getting at something, a cold austerity or refusal in Godard's style, but she is ignoring the warmth around the edges. We also know now, from his later work, that Godard's documentary, fact-hungry impulse always contained a fair amount of sociological curiosity.

Her longer piece, "Godard" (1968), which appeared in her second collection, *Styles of Radical Will*, is more successful at recognizing and reconciling the contradictions in the filmmaker. This essay is a triumphant piece of hero-worship. She continues to champion Godard as the model for her preferred aesthetic: purist, ascetic, aleatoric, hybridizing, antipsychological, fragmented. But she also appreciates his claim to offer no more than "efforts or attempts" as a sign that he is an essayist at heart—like her. "Godard has elaborated a largely anti-poetic cinema, one of whose chief literary models is the prose essay. Godard has even said: 'I consider myself an essay writer. I write essays in the form of novels, or novels in the form of essays'" (SRW, 155). Having gone that far, she also quotes Godard's statement that "we novelists and filmmakers are condemned to an analysis of the world, of the real; painters and musicians aren't." So by 1968 Godard at least, if not Sontag herself, has accepted the burden and necessity of analysis, interpretation.

Sontag is clearly on firm modernist ground in her long Godard essay, and the result is as surefooted as it is helpful. But I am more moved, in a way, by her essay on *Persona*, perhaps because Ingmar Bergman was not then a favorite of film buffs. *Persona*, an ambiguous masterpiece about two women locked in a power struggle, obviously fascinated and affected Sontag. She used the then-prevalent device of attacking other, more benighted film critics to frame her own critique. Having sorted through the loose ends of the plot, she wrote: "Such reduction to a story means, in the end, a reduction of Bergman's film to the single dimension of psychology. Not that the psychological dimension isn't there. It is. But to understand *Persona*, the viewer must go beyond the psychological point of view. . . . *Persona* takes a position beyond psychology—as it does, in an analogous sense, beyond eroticism" (SRW, 130–31). It would be hard to deny the psychological or erotic dimensions in this particular movie, and Sontag knows she can't—one suspects they are what hold her in thrall—but she makes a conscientious effort, meanwhile bringing to light numerous subtleties of that mysterious film.

By her third collection, *Under the Sign of Saturn*, she had begun to pull away from movie love. In her 1979 essay on "Syberberg's Hitler," she wrote: "For whatever Syberberg says, cinema is now another lost paradise. In the era of cinema's unprecedented mediocrity, his masterpiece has something of the character of a posthumous event" (USS, 163). That supposedly "mediocre" era, give or take five years, saw the making of Antonioni's *The Passenger*, Tarkovsky's *Stalker*, Woody Allen's *Manhattan*, Scorsese's *Raging Bull*, Marker's *Sans Soleil*, Wiseman's *Welfare*, Lanzmann's *Shoah*, Truffaut's *The Green Room*, Bresson's *L'Argent*, Akerman's *Jeanne Dielman*, Angelopoulos's *The Traveling Players*, Cassavetes' *Opening Night*, Bergman's *Fanny and Alexander*, Rohmer's *The Aviator's Wife*, Oshima's *In the Realm of the Senses*, Imamura's *Vengeance Is Mine*, Malick's *Days of Heaven*, Coppola's *Apocalypse Now*, Bunuel's *That Obscure Object of Desire*, Altman's *Nashville*, Fassbinder's *The Marriage of Maria Braun*, Bertolucci's *Last Tango in Paris*, Pialat's *A Nos Amours*,. . . That's a lot of "posthumous events." Still to come would be the masterworks of Almodovar, Sokurov, Hou, Kiarostami, Leigh, Miyazawa, Herzog, and so on.

By 1995, in her essay "A Century of Cinema," she was declaring that "movies are dead." They have gone into "an ignominious, irreversible decline. This doesn't mean that there won't be any more new films one can admire. But such films will not simply be exceptions; that's true of great achievement in any art. They will have to be heroic violations of the norms and practices which now govern moviemaking everywhere in the capitalist and would-be capitalist world—

which is to say, everywhere" (WSF, 117). Heroic violations or no, there are more than enough admirable new films each year to oversupply annual ten-best lists since 1995. I don't dispute that the early sixties were a marvelous and perhaps unparalleled outpouring for world cinema, and I can understand her regret at the lessening of that flood; that doesn't mean that cinema today is dead.

Sontag's lament sounds a good deal like intellectual film critics of the 1930s who, faced with the coming of sound and the increasingly industrial nature of film production, would write, as Rudolf Arnheim did in his 1935 essay "The Film Critic of Tomorrow": "Formerly, good films differed from mediocre ones only insofar as their quality was concerned; today, they are outsiders, remnants, things of a basically different nature from that which normally passes through the cinemas. . . . [The critic] thinks he is seeing bad films instead of understanding that what he sees is no longer film at all."* A few decades later, in the late sixties, Godard also pronounced cinema dying or dead. More recently, Paul Schrader has questioned whether it any longer makes sense to

---

* Reprinted in *American Movie Critics* (Library of America, 2008), 92.

put forth a cinematic canon when the art form itself faces extinction, to be replaced by digitized hand-gadgets. These concerns are valid, and I think Sontag started, or restarted, a useful discussion by phrasing the problem as direly as she did. It was also, of course, another instance of her reverting to the "crisis" mode in framing an argument.

For Sontag, watching a movie had become too easy; it lacked agon. With a few exceptions: "Syberberg's unprecedented ambition in *Hitler: A Film from Germany* is on another scale from anything one has seen on film. It is work that requires a special kind of attention and partisanship; and invites being reflected upon, reseen. . . . As was said ruefully of Wagner, he spoils our tolerance for the others" (USS, 165). Sontag's championing of extra-long German films can be traced to her growing appetite for *Gesamtkunstwerk* on the Wagnerian scale (the *Ring* itself, and Robert Wilson's productions, such as *Einstein on the Beach*, which she boasted of having sat through more than a dozen times). About *Hitler*, she wrote. "Its length is suitably exhaustive—seven hours; and, like the *Ring*, it is a tetralogy" (USS, 140–41). Even more "suitably exhaustive" was Fassbinder's fifteen-hour-plus *Berlin Alexanderplatz*. She seemed to rate an artwork in direct proportion to the number of hours it took to experience it. She was demonstrating, as she said about Artaud, a "taste for spiritual and physical effort—for art as an ordeal" (USS, 33). She had become the Queen of Sitzfleish.*

Another reason why, I think, Sontag abandoned the writing of film criticism is that she began making her own four feature films. While many directors have started off as film critics, it is almost unheard-of for any to return to writing criticism once they have turned out a few pictures themselves. There must be, in the experience of raising funds, mounting a production, collaborating with a crew and shooting, so deep an engagement with grubby practicalities and contingencies out of one's control that it becomes impossible to view movies again with the same innocent clarity of the film critic.

My Favorite Book of Hers

🔳 My favorite book of Sontag's—not necessarily her best book but the one I like best—is *Under the Sign of Saturn*. I like it partly because

---

* A Yiddish word meaning the ability to apply one's posterior to the seat for as long as it takes.

it is free of the aggressive, badgering tone of her aesthetic polemics, and is instead a fairly unified suite of sympathetic biographical portraits of male melancholics, her heroes of the intellect (Paul Goodman, Antonin Artaud, Roland Barthes, Walter Benjamin, Hans-Jurgen Syberberg, Elias Canetti), with the one gender exception being Leni Riefensthal in "Fascinating Fascism," which is not at all sympathetic but brilliant in other ways. I don't think it is incorrect to say that Sontag was essentially male-identified; she wrote much more sympathetically and readily about men than about women, which landed her in trouble at times with feminist critics. Nor would I put it past myself to have liked these biographical essays of *luftmenschen* so much, partly for the reason that as a male reader I identify more strongly with them.

What she admired, or envied, about these men was not only their intellectual achievement but their melancholy solitude, which allowed them to keep the world at bay and get on with their work. Benjamin was the quintessential isolate bachelor, despite his failed early marriage; Goodman, though he had a wife and kids, was gay and a restless cruiser, given (as he put it in his diary *Five Years*) to looking for love in places where it couldn't be found; Artaud was too crazy for the calm rhythms and accords of domestic life; Barthes lived with his mother until she died, then by himself; Canetti was married but a philandering scholar who ate up whole libraries. Sontag commented often on how difficult it was for a woman writer to appropriate the oceans of alone-time that every writer needs, since women tend to become more entangled in domestic responsibilities and are expected to be care-givers.

Craig Seligman, in *Sontag & Kael*, conjectures that Sontag was also a depressive, which is why she wrote so sympathetically about melancholia. We now have the proof from no less an authority than her son, David Rieff, in his memoir, *Swimming in a Sea of Death*, that "she was almost always dueling with depression. This was clearest immediately after she woke up, when, in an effort to shake off her despondency, she would talk, about anything and at breakneck speed, as if to overwhelm her mood with meteor showers of verbiage" (139). That description recalls her own depiction of the Cavaliere in *The Volcano Lover*: "His is the hyperactivity of the heroic depressive. He ferried himself past one vortex of melancholy after another by means of an astonishing spread of enthusiasms" (VL, 20).

Beyond her own experiences with melancholy, I also think she romanticized male depression as an aristocratic retreat. The roots of that tenderness toward male melancholics may have links to the early death of her father, Jack Rosenblatt, in China: she was only six at the time, and I take that event to have left a lifelong wound, in much the same sense that Edmund Wilson writes about the early fructifying traumas of various writers in *The Wound and The Bow*. The autobiographical "Project for a Trip to China," one of Sontag's best stories in *I, etcetera*, speaks directly about this loss. "My father, tubercular, never came back from China" (IE, 17). "I still weep in any movie with a scene in which the father returns home from a long desperate absence, at the moment that he hugs his child. Or children" (IE, 11). "It is oppressive to have an invisible father." "I shall forgive my father. For dying."

She addresses the moment when she learned of the death from her mother (called M. in the story): "After M. returned to the United States from China in early 1939, it took several months for her to tell me my father wasn't coming back. . . . I didn't cry long. I was already imagining how I would announce this new fact to my friends. I was sent out to play. I didn't really believe my father was dead. . . . I am six years old. My grief falls like snowflakes" (IE, 24–25). The working-out of that grief may have had another result, as she reports in the same story: "Somewhere, some place inside myself, I am detached. I have always been detached (in part). Always" (IE, 24). It is this detachment, flecked with grief, that she enthusiastically examines in the studies that make up *Under the Sign of Saturn*.

The collection opens with "On Paul Goodman," an immensely appealing personal essay. She is sitting in a "tiny room in Paris," surrounded by books and manuscripts, trying "to make a new start." News has reached her of the death of Paul Goodman. "The grief I feel at Paul Goodman's death is sharper because we were not friends, though we co-inhabited several of the same worlds" (USS, 4). This will partly be the story of a failed friendship between two audacious thinkers. Why were they not friends? "I disliked him—the reason being, as I often explained plaintively during his lifetime, that I felt he didn't like me. How pathetic and merely formal that dislike was I always knew" (USS, 5). Sontag shows a very human side here: vulnerable to others' dislike, particularly the dislike of respected elders. She found him "mildly rude . . . cold and self-absorbed. . . . I was told by mutual friends that he didn't really like women as people—though he made an exception for a few particular women, of course" (USS, 4–5). Still, he had been her hero: "It was that voice that seduced me—that direct, cranky, egotistical, generous American voice. . . . Paul Goodman's voice touched everything he wrote about with intensity, interest, and his own terribly appealing sureness and awkwardness" (USS, 6). Gone are the gnomic European tones in her own voice as priestess-demystifier; nothing could be more transparent, more candidly American. We perceive that another influential national prose model, besides the French or German, has been operating in her head.

By his polymath example as a poet/playwright/ social critic Goodman gave consent to try many things, just as Sontag aspired to write novels and shoot films and direct theatre alongside her essays. He also led the way in "being an academic freeloader and an outlaw psychiatrist," (USS, 7) outside the university walls. "His so-called amateurism is identical with his genius: that amateurism enabled him to bring to the questions of schooling, psychiatry, and citizenship an extraordinary, curmudgeonly accuracy of insight and freedom to envisage practical change" (USS, 8). Finally, he gave her the courage to badger in a straightforward, social-critic way, as Barthes never could. She ends the essay by saying how hard it will be to go on "without Paul's hectoring, without Paul's patient meandering explanations of everything, without the grace of Paul's example" (USS, 10). In her rising above his personal rudeness toward her and celebrating his virtues (including hectoring) with grace and generosity, she sets a fine example.

The second piece in the collection is one of Sontag's most intellectually ambitious. "Approaching Artaud" is aptly named because she spends the whole essay circling her subject, Antonin Artaud, from different perspectives: first, a prologue about the "death-of-the-author" crisis in modernism, extending back as always to Nietzsche, in this case his call for the "transvaluation of all values;" second, surrealism, which both welcomed and repelled Artaud; third, a biography of the mad, failed, suffering theatre visionary; fourth, an examination of his call for a theatre of ritual, stripped of dialogue and individual psychology; fifth, the enduring influence of his ideas in experimental theatre today, and their coextension with current topical fads, including shamanism, Oriental religions, trance, drugs, magic; sixth, an inquiry into the connections between Gnosticism and schizophrenia, and the incompatibility between the individual at his most antisocial, or mad, and humanist liberal democracy; and seventh, the ultimately "unassimilable" nature of Artaud's "voice and presence," for all their trendy allure. She concludes:

> He is an example of a willed classic—an author whom the culture attempts to assimilate but who remains profoundly undigestible. One use of literary respectability in our time—and an important part of the complex career of literary modernism—is to make acceptable an outrageous, essentially forbidding author, who becomes a classic on the basis of the many interesting things to be said about the work that scarcely convey (perhaps even conceal) the real nature of the work itself, which may be, among other things, extremely boring or morally monstrous or terribly painful to read. Sade, Artaud, and Wilhelm Reich belong in this company: authors who were jailed or locked up in insane asylums because they were screaming, because they were out of control; immoderate, obsessed, strident authors who repeat themselves endlessly, who are rewarding to quote and read bits of, but who overpower and exhaust if read in large quantities. (USS, 69–70)

But she has read Artaud, and digested him, and saved us the trouble of doing so, and she is not above complimenting herself for her effort. Fair enough.

The problem with the essay, serious and searching as it is, is that it seems overly long for its payoff. Maybe Artaud was too extreme, too much of a nut, to pin all these ideas onto. The result is like being trapped in the circularities and tautologies of a crazy brain. "Only the exhausting is truly interesting," she declares—a wonderful Sontagian aphorism, but like most aphorisms, no more than partly true. Perhaps it really was true for her?

In line with this preference for "the exhausting" was her insistence that only the haters, the obsessive ranters, were relevant to the cultural crisis of late modernism. She began her Simone Weil essay in *Against Interpretation* by writing:

> The culture-heroes of our liberal bourgeois civilization are anti-liberal and anti-bourgeois; they are writers who are repetitive, obsessive, and impolite, who impress by force—not simply by their tone of personal authority and by their intellectual ardor, but by the sense of acute personal and intellectual extremity. The bigots, the hysterics, the destroyers of the self—these

are the writers who bear witness to the fearful polite time in which we live. (AI, 49)

She made this assertion a number of times, explaining the importance of Thomas Bernhard, Celine, Artaud, Beckett—the progeny of Dostoyevsky's *Notes From Underground*. I think she was right in identifying the obsessive-rant narration as a significant offshoot in modernist writing, perhaps a way of circumventing the scene-and-dialogue conventions of realist fiction, which seemed played-out to her. But I think she was wrong in saying its practitioners were the only ones that counted in contemporary culture. It's like saying that only the boring or fanatical are interesting. Yes, up to a point, but . . . no. Sontag herself expresses qualms, in the same Simone Weil essay, while going on to resolve them: "I, for one, do not doubt that the sane view of the world is the true one. But is that what is always wanted, truth? The need for truth is not constant; no more than is the need for repose. An idea which is a distortion may have a greater intellectual thrust than the truth; it may better serve the needs of the spirit, which vary. The truth is balance, but the opposite of truth, which is unbalance, may not be a lie" (AI, 50).

I am much more drawn to balance as a goal than Sontag was, which is why Montaigne remains my essayistic ideal and she rarely mentions him. I also am more put off by insanity and hysteria (perhaps I've seen too much of them in my life) to glamorize them as promising distortions, the way she did. But the idea of madness as occult knowledge was very much in the air when Sontag wrote her Weil and Artaud essays: R. D. Laing's *The Divided Self*, for instance, argued that schizophrenia was a sensible way-station on the road to integration, that one needed to "go through" the craziness, just as LSD users claimed that you must lose your mind in order to gain it, or the movie *King of Hearts* premised that lunacy was an appropriate adaptive response to a mad society. Sontag's film *Brother Carl* was a muddled attempt to give these concepts dramatic form, while trying to approximate the austerely morbid spiritual atmosphere of Dreyer's *Ordet* (in both, a disturbed family member tries to raise the dead).

The title essay on Walter Benjamin, "Under the Sign of Saturn," is my favorite in the book, and probably my favorite of all her essays. Her tribute is a rare act of sympathy by which one author assimilates another, and transmits unselfishly that spirit to the reader, rendering his notoriously difficult aspects into something coherent and attractive. The key is her explication of melancholia (Saturn being the astrological sign of melancholics), as fundamental to Benjamin's work.

The prose is dense but clear, never stuffy or derivative; one would have to quote the entire Sontag essay to convey its method of piling idea upon idea, so that each insight builds on all the previous ones. A few sentences, extracted from the middle, may suffice:

> Benjamin's recurrent themes are, characteristically, means of spatializing the world: for example, his notion of ideas and experiences as ruins. To understand something is to understand its topography, to know how to chart it. And to know how to get lost. For the character born under the sign of Saturn, time is the medium of constraint, inadequacy, repetition, mere fulfillment. In time, one is only what one is: what one has always been. In space, one can be another person. Benjamin's poor sense of direction and inability to read a street map became his love of travel and his mastery of the art of straying. Time does not give one much leeway: it thrusts us forward from

behind, blows us through the narrow funnel of the present into the future. But space is broad, teeming with possibilities, positions, intersections, passages, detours, U-turns, dead ends, one-way streets. Too many possibilities, indeed. Since the Saturnine temperament is slow, prone to indecisiveness, sometimes one has to cut one's way through with a knife. Sometimes one ends by turning the knife against oneself. (USS, 116–17)

Anyone familiar with Benjamin's work will hear echoes and paraphrases here: for instance, he dedicated his collage of reflections, "One Way Street," to Asja Lacis, "who cut it through the author." Sontag's prose here is also remarkably rhythmic, as though she were in a semi-trance when composing it, able to channel Benjamin's spirit calmly while looking at him objectively. The probing way she reads and understands Benjamin would seem a vindication of that very psychological method she elsewhere disdains. She is aware of the contradiction, saying: "One cannot use the life to interpret the work. But one can use the work to interpret the life" (USS, 111).

She begins novelistically, by describing Benjamin as he appears in photographs. Then she takes us through some of his dominant motifs and characteristics: topography, miniaturization, indecisiveness, keeping one's options open, a courtier's courtesy. Benjamin was a passionate collector, and in her analysis of his fidelity to things ("The more lifeless things are, the more potent and ingenious can be the mind which contemplates them" [USS, 120]), we get a first glimpse of the Cavaliere, the collector-protagonist of her novel *The Volcano Lover*. Benjamin was also another exemplar for her of "the freelance intellectual." Finally, he was a negative model in the difficulty he had finishing books. "His characteristic form remained the essay. The melancholic's intensity and exhaustiveness of attention set natural limits to the length at which Benjamin could develop his ideas. His major essays seem to end just in time, before they self-destruct." Her own essay on Benjamin runs a mere twenty-five pages. She later said, by way of explaining why she no longer gave her main energies to essay writing, that some of the essays in *Under the Sign of Saturn* had taken her six months to write. From my perspective, this means she should have persisted in essay writing; it was just getting to the proper level of difficulty.

"Fascinating Fascism," on Leni Riefenstahl, is one of her signature essays, and a great one. Sontag was of that last, now dying-off generation, for whom Fascism remained a living threat, not a piece of nostalgia for the History Channel. "Fascinating Fascism" was her attempt to deal with that moment when Fascism as palpable evil was slipping into oblivion, its demonic menace becoming campy, like a Halloween costume. Pasolini had already dealt provocatively, in *Salo*, and Visconti, somewhat more floridly and less honestly, in *The Damned*, with the aestheticization of sadomasochism within a Fascist context; now it was her turn.

Sontag is scornful of Riefenstahl's lies and "misinformation," and appalled by attempts to rehabilitate her as an innocent. She portrays Leni as a pretty, manipulative woman who retreats behind false naivete and love of beauty when it suits her. Sontag heaps scorn on her sisters who still celebrate Riefenstahl:

> Part of the impetus behind Riefenstahl's recent promotion to the status of a cultural monument surely owes to the fact that she is a woman. The 1973 New York Film Festival poster, made by a well-known artist who is also a feminist, showed a blonde doll-woman whose right breast is encircled by three names: Agnes Leni Shirley. (That is, Varda, Riefenstahl, Clarke.) Feminists would feel a pang at having to sacri-

fice the one woman who made films that everyone acknowledges to be first-rate. (USS, 84)

"Fascinating Fascism" appeared in 1974, when
Sontag had already begun the essays which
would comprise *On Photography*, and both texts
worry the morality of photographed images and
demonstrate a prosecutorial tone. "Fascinating
Fascism" literally uses the device "Exhibit A,"
"Exhibit B" to structure her indictment, like a dis-
trict attorney. The essay's power derives in large
measure from the controlled fury underneath its
calm laying-out of facts and exhibits. Of course
there are glints of unfair argumentation here and
there, such as when Sontag makes the intuitively
plausible (but finally overreaching) inference
that Riefenstahl's lavishly captured athletic bodies in motion in *Olympia* are but another expression of Fascism, or that her loving portraits of
the Nuba tribesman are also Fascist and racist at
their core. Still, we are with Sontag, 99 percent of
us, urging her on, because this time she is attacking Nazis, and so a little unfairness never hurts.
We hold our breaths as we watch Sontag go to it,
with a rhetorical power rare in this day and age.
Not only does Sontag take on Riefenstahl and her
defenders, her own friends at the Telluride and
New York Film Festivals, and fellow feminists,

she also takes on herself, or her past views, with gritty determination.

In the 1965 essay "On Style" she had written:

> To call Leni Riefenstahl's *The Triumph of the Will* and *The Olympiad* masterpieces is not to gloss over Nazi propaganda with aesthetic lenience. The Nazi propaganda is there. But something else is there, too, which we reject at our loss. Because they project the complex movements of intelligence and grace and sensuousness, these two films of Riefenstahl (unique among Nazi artists) transcend the categories of propaganda or even reportage. And we find ourselves—to be sure, rather uncomfortably— seeing 'Hitler' and not Hitler, the '1936 Olympics' and not the 1936 Olympics. Through Riefenstahl's genius as a film-maker, the content has—let us even assume, against her intentions—come to play a purely formal role. (AI, 25–26)

Now she is having none of it. Now she is saying: "To cast Riefenstahl as the individualist-artist, defying philistine bureaucrats and censorship by the patron state ... should seem like nonsense to anyone who has seen *Triumph of the Will*—a film whose very conception negates the possibility of the filmmaker's having an aesthetic conception independent of propaganda" (USS, 79).

In "Fascinating Fascism" she also distances herself from her earlier discussion on pornography, where she seemed to be arguing that everything in the imagination is permitted, to a position that stresses the moral problem of the unfettered sexual instinct. "How could a regime which persecuted homosexuals become a gay turn-on?" she demands (USS, 102). Here she questions the limits of camp, much more so than she did in her pioneering exploration of that phenomenon. The essay ends with this no-holds-barred paragraph:

> Sadomasochism has always been the furthest reach of the sexual experience: when sex becomes most purely sexual, that is, severed from personhood, from relationships, from love. It should not be surprising that it has become attached to Nazi symbolism in recent years. Never before was the relation of masters and slaves so consciously aestheticized. Sade had to make up his theatre of punishment and delight from scratch, improvising the décor and costumes and blasphemous rites. Now there is a master scenario available to everyone. The color is black, the material is leather, the seduction

is beauty, the justification is honesty, the aim is ecstasy, the fantasy is death. (USS, 105)

That last sentence is a marvel. Still the master of aphorisms, of the passive-verb sentence in declarative mode, but the prose itself could not be clearer. In combatively taking on this important subject, Sontag purged herself of the aura of "difficulty" that had previously made some readers feel they were not quite up to the task.

Readers Feeling Stupid

I have often heard acquaintances or graduate students, some of the most intelligent, say that when they read Susan Sontag, they felt stupid. As one thoughtful writer-friend put it, "I feel as if I have one brain and she has two." They seemed to be basing this impression partly on Sontag's vast range of cultural and philosophical references, and partly on their struggle to figure out the meaning or emotional drift underneath some of her more impersonal sentences. But I also think it part of her strategy to make the reader feel stupid. She did that occasionally by a calculated use of obscure references ("Philo of Alexandria"), but more often by a prose style that tended toward opaqueness, and kept promising more resolution or clarity than it delivered. I am not saying she wanted to give pain to the common reader (though she may have); she may also have been trying to give pleasure to the more sophisticated reader, by trying to imitate the way Barthes flattered the educated reader by leaving out obvious transitions. The difference between the way Barthes did it and the way Sontag does it is that Barthes is unfailingly genial in his assertions, which often point courtier-like in two directions of meaning, whereas Sontag's assertions are more blunt and truculent. They stake a claim, then refuse to elaborate, leaving many readers feeling like dumb yokels.

(I would qualify that by saying that Sontag can also be the clearest of writers, illuminating difficult ideas without leaving a shred of confusion behind. What I am calling her "opaque" manner was particularly in evidence over the first essay collections and in *On Photography*; her late manner became looser and more conversational, closer to the mode of a speech. Since she was often called upon to give addresses, she developed a prose style that was more oral and vernacular for those occasions, and then either she found she could no longer go back to the earlier, gnomic style, or else she felt she had exhausted its uses. In these later writings, you are invited to feel stupid not by a blur of aphoristic language but by the reader's presumed lack of cultural depth in relation to the author.)

One of Sontag's strategies from the beginning was to claim that the author or work she was bringing before the reader had been shamefully neglected; and she, by implication, was going to right that injustice with her appreciation. Neglected, yes, as is most art, but by whom and how much? Robert Bresson? Machado de Assis? Victor Serge? Robert Walser? These were hardly unknown quantities in the film or literature worlds when she wrote her essays about them. They may not have been household names in America, but that does not mean they were ignored in American intellectual-academic discourse. Bresson's films were distributed and reviewed respectfully, his *Trial of Joan of Arc* had premiered in the first New York Film Festival; all the major and most of the minor titles of Machado de Assis had been translated and published by the time her essay appeared; there had been a Victor Serge vogue in the late sixties, periodically recurring thereafter. So it was only by addressing the "philistine" American audience, those readers she was trying to make feel stupid—or better yet, the readers who had begun to catch some references and thereby felt good about not belonging to the philistines, while still intellectually insecure and therefore needing to heed Sontag—that she could make stick the claim of shameful neglect.

This is not in any way to discount the good she did by spreading the word about worthy, important artists. In her efforts to popularize difficult art, she functioned as a missionary of culture, and a generous one. If I may not sound sufficiently grateful, it is because I, being only ten years younger than Sontag and belonging roughly to the same intellectual class, already knew something of her subjects when her appreciations appeared. So, while I esteemed her take on them, which was often brilliant, I did not appreciate the hectoring, guilt-inducing tone about neglect in which they were packaged. Nor could I accept, the way a much younger person might, the entire frame of reference as coming from her, because it was in the very air we both breathed.

The writers, artists, and intellectuals whom Sontag saw it as her mission to introduce to the American public were generally Europeans, who produced work hard to digest, work which, in her words, "demands special effort" (AI, 295). They were not, in the main, obscure, but important figures in the common currency of international culture—stars abroad though not here. I remember going into a large bookstore the first time I visited Paris, in 1964, and seeing titles by Walter Benjamin, Georges Bataille, Georg Lukacs, E. M. Cioran, Antonin Artaud, Michel Leiris, and Simone Weil, all laid out on the most prominent tables. It was as though I were staring at Sontag's agenda of topics. And she made no bones about the fact that she was acting as a trend-spotter, bringing the doltish Americans up to speed with what everyone else already knew. Her early essays were peppered with phrases appealing to the reader's appetite for intellectual fashion: Lukacs "has a special eminence and claim to our attention" and "he has counted for a long time" (AI, 83); Claude Levi-Strauss and his followers "have a claim on our interest" (AI, 70); Nathalie Sarraute points the way to a new novel that "people with serious and sophisticated taste in the other arts can take seriously" (AI, 111). In short, we should read what she has to say on X because X has already been adjudged important, has a "claim on our interest," the "our" being those in the know, and if you want to be one of those in the know, you had better find out what they/we are talking about.

Granted, it is a common essayistic strategy for cultural critics to try to catch the attention of readers by insisting that what they are about to explicate, however much it may have passed under the radar of pop culture, is VERY IMPORTANT. I also don't mean to poke anti-intellectual fun at Sontag's rigorous heroes of the mind, since I consider the figures she wrote about significant as well. What I object to is not her writing about them, but the slightly bullying tone she took, and the somewhat crude way she played on her intellectually upwardly mobile readers' insecurities. The blatancy of that appeal became more striking when she functioned as a sort of freelance advance scout for *Vogue* and other fashion magazines, telling readers that they needed to rush out to the latest seven-hour masterwork. Space limitations in the slicks clipped the subtle argumentation of her best essays, and these pieces came across largely as consumer tips.

Craig Seligman, in *Sontag & Kael*, makes a sweet attempt to defend Sontag from criticism that she was a "fashionista" by characterizing these labels as sexist. But the fact remains that she *was* very attuned to the hip, the hot, the au courant. She was a celebrity in her own right, and for that very reason alone may have been more fascinated with the mechanism of celebrity. When she traveled to different countries, she would ask the local literati: Who are your new writers who really *matter*? Even when she was dying, she wanted to be the first to spread the word that the Chilean writer Roberto Bolaño was "the real thing and the rarest . . ." And she was right about Bolaño: he *is* marvelous. One can see this "fashionista" tendency in a negative light, as an insecure need to be always on the cutting edge, or, in a positive light, as a demonstration of her curiosity and unquenchable enthusiasm for making new discoveries.

The Benefactor

🔲 As discussed earlier, Sontag had no interest in writing a traditional, "square" realist novel when she began her forays into fiction. She was drawn to the "unreliable-narrator" tradition, which was very much in the air at the time. It may help to consider the cultural milieu when her first novel was being written. Around Columbia, where she taught and I went to school, there were vogues in the early sixties for Italo Svevo and Machado de Assis (both championed by the poet Kenneth Koch, also on the faculty, in his Comic Literature course); Herman Hesse's *Steppenwolf*; Gide's *The Immoralist*; Camus' *The Stranger*; Ford's *The Good Soldier*; and James Purdy's *Malcolm*, among others. *The Benefactor* displays the stylized élan of this particular family of books.

Its narrator-hero, Hipployte, is clearly not autobiographical, save perhaps for a sliver of detached superiority and youthful intrepidity. He sports a reflective, aphoristic intelligence, and many of the best passages in the novel are, as one might imagine, essayistic digressions—but overall, he just doesn't realize what he's saying. This is first-person comedy of self-delusion.

In her beautiful essay on Machado de Assis, another of Sontag's male loners, Sontag gives a blueprint for the kind of novel she was trying to write. Though she insists that she had not yet encountered Machado's work when she wrote *The Benefactor*, she was certainly familiar with "the tradition on narrative buffoonery" it belonged to, which she astutely summarizes in her Machado essay as follows:

> The talkative first-person voice attempting to ingratiate itself with readers—which runs from Sterne through, in our own century, Natsume Soseki's *I Am a Cat*, the short fiction of Robert Walser, Svevo's *Confessions of Zeno* and *As a Man Grows Older*, Hrabal's *Too Loud a Solitude*, much of Beckett. Again and again we meet in different guises the chatty, meandering, compulsively

speculative, eccentric narrator: reclusive (by choice or by vocation); prone to futile obsessions and fanciful theories and comically designed efforts of the will; often an autodidact; not quite a crank; though sometimes driven by lust, and at least one time by love, unable to mate; usually elderly; invariably male. (No woman is likely to get even the conditional sympathy these ragingly self-absorbed narrators claim from us, because of expectations that women be more sympathetic, and sympathizing, than men; a woman with the same degree of mental acuity and emotional separateness would be regarded simply as a monster). (WSF, 35)

This last point is especially shrewd, and points to why Sontag chose so often to write about male protagonists in her fiction. She could entertain the fantasy of solipsism and its mental freedom, which intrigued her, while critiquing it as a male affectation. In any case, *The Benefactor* incorporates all the characteristics of the "narrative buffoon" she has listed above. I share Sontag's love of this mischievous tradition; it has shaped me as a writer, and so I began reading *The Benefactor* with high hopes. The first chapter is delightful, very promising. It recreates that Svevoesque, rationalizing tone of the eccentric narrator and amateur philosopher. The protagonist tells his well-to-do father that he has abandoned his formal studies. Note the bookish, antiquarian, slightly formal tone of literature in translation, a manner Sontag has perfectly mimicked.

> To my great satisfaction, he was not angry. According to his view, my older brother had fulfilled all the hopes he had for a son; for this reason he declared himself willing to support me in any independent path I might choose. He made arrangements with his banker to increase my monthly allowance, and we parted warmly with assurances of his continued affection. I was now in the enviable position of being entirely at my own disposal, free to pursue my own questions (the treasure I had accumulated since my childhood) and to satisfy, better than any university had done, my passion for speculation and investigation. (TB, 6)

The absence of money worries will clear a space for mental adventures. There are no romantic worries, either, since the protagonist is irresistibly attractive to women, and moreover has no particular desire to fall in love and marry. Having boxed herself in this way, Sontag can think of no further plot variation than to turn Hippolyte into a pander for his and others' sexual experimentation. The book becomes dry and boring, because nothing for the hero is finally at risk. Hippolyte is as close to an invulnerable character as possible: he has rude health, money, lacks ambition, is not driven by passion. The only thing he cares about is his dreams. He can't get beyond himself: he is in a vicious circle. The author's bravery is in insisting on the allure of solipsism. "I submit that I made a choice, admittedly an unusual one. I chose myself. And because of my absorption in myself and relative indifference to other people, my inward ear became acute enough to hear a mandate from myself which isolated me from others. The mandate was, so far as I understand it, to live out to the fullest the meaning of privacy" (TB, 272). All very intriguing, theoretically, but the plot is dramatically dead on arrival, since the novelist has failed (or refused) to equip her character with any desire.

In the long run, it is hard to sustain interest in a novel whose protagonist desires nothing serious (to hold onto his night dreams long enough to live in them during the day isn't serious, but a sort of surrealist conceit). The book comes sporadically alive only through the desires of the women characters (Frau Anders, Monique) for the hero. He wants only to flee their grasp, and once he has successfully done so, we are back to square one. Hippolyte is, in short, empty. He is hardly in a position to be anyone's benefactor. He meddles in people's lives, ruining them. He sells his mistress into slavery, even tries to kill her. (The plot turns into opera farce, like *Abduction of the Seraglio*, and flirts with slapstick and pornography, which does not make the novel any more emotionally engaging.)* For all his rationales about granting his mistress freedom, Hippolye is a monster, incapable of learning anything, and I think meant to be seen as such. Hence the title's irony. But irony is not humor, and Sontag's inadequate comic resources, in a genre that puts a

---

* As Sontag herself shrewdly observed, in "The Pornographic Imagination" (1967): "[Sade's] Justine is like Candide, who is also a cipher, a blank , an eternal naif incapable of learning anything from his atrocious ordeals. The familiar structure of comedy which features a character who is a still center in the midst of outrage (Buster Keaton is a classic image) crops up repeatedly in pornography. . . . Silent film comedy offers many illustrations of how the formal principle of continual agitation or perpetual motion (slapstick) and that of deadpan really converge to the same end—a deadening or neutralization or distancing of the audience's emotions, its ability to identify in a 'humane' way and to make moral judgments about situations of violence. The same principle is at work in all pornography. It's not that the characters in pornography cannot conceivably possess any emotions. They can. But the principles of under-reacting and frenetic agitation make the emotional climate self-canceling, so that the basic tone of pornography is affectless, emotionless" (RW, 54–55).

premium on humor and mischief, finally dooms the book.

Humor and Seriousness

🔲 It was often said by critics, such as Eliot Weinberger in the *New York Review of Books*, that Susan Sontag was "utterly humorless." This statement, for the most part true, still needs qualification. Sontag the aphorist did have a strong acerbic wit, which in a pinch could be taken for humor. Her command of a range of ironic tones was indisputable. The aggressiveness of her provocative stances might also be seen as a starting-point for a humor rooted in surprise. Though atypical, her descriptions of sci-fi movies in "The Imagination of Disaster" show a gusto for absurdist detail. She also valued and admired comic writers, such as Lawrence Sterne, Machado de Assis, Donald Barthelme—in short, she knew what the stuff looked like, had a theoretical understanding of humor, just couldn't do it well herself. A number of her short stories in *I, Etc.* ("American Spirits" and "Baby") and her first novel, *The Benefactor*, clearly *mean* to be comic but they are painfully mirthless performances. She lacked the vivacity, the *sprezzatura*, to pull off these fanciful baubles, and beyond that, she lacked a talent or goodwill for giving readers the pleasurable release that all comic masters know how to orchestrate. Whether that lack issued from an austere refusal to oblige the bourgeois reader, or a willingness to amuse but the inability to do so, I am not sure: possibly a combination of both. Overall, Sontag either didn't know how to give pleasure in fiction—or wouldn't. She was too hooked on the puritanical notion of art as ordeal, until she came to write *The Volcano Lover*.

The novelist Sigrid Nunez, who had been David Rieff's girlfriend and had lived under Sontag's roof for years as a sort of daughter-in-law in training, wrote a memorial essay in which she took strenuous issue with the idea that Sontag had no sense of humor. I am willing to stand corrected, even if in my own encounters I do not remember ever being moved to laughter by a thing she said. Yet there was that heartiness of hers that sometimes mimicked the comic spirit, and occasionally she let fly a cruel, contemptuous chortle that did suggest she had a funny-bone, however dismayingly or inappropriately it manifested. She had, let us conclude, a weak sense of humor, which rarely revealed itself on the page.

In later years, Sontag saw herself as the last angry champion of "seriousness" (it became her catchword, her fetish-term) in a culture that had forgotten how to be so. There is no innate contradiction between being serious and having a marvelous sense of humor. She asserted as much in her Nadine Gordimer lecture, defining "Be serious" as meaning "Never be cynical. And which *doesn't* preclude being funny" (ATST, 211). But for Sontag, in practice if not in theory, the two seemed irreconcilable. "Serious" was her war cry sounded in retreat for a battle deemed already lost; "serious" was a dead language only she and a few others (Sebald, Syberberg) still spoke; "serious" was a Watteauesque isle of cerebral *fêtes galantes* all but fallen into the sea, soon to become as fabled and dubious as Atlantis. As she did with "greatness," Sontag used the word so frequently and imprecisely in her last years that it drained of all meaning, and came to stand only, like a mirror, for herself and her endorsements.

Death Kit

If *The Benefactor* was an aridly ludic attempt to merge *Candide*-like narrative buffoonery with surrealism, *Death Kit* is a slog through dimly lit tunnel vision, a third-person recounting of the limited mental perspective of one protagonist.

The author's attitude toward her protagonist can best be described as snide. She gives him the boy-man nickname Diddy, and describes him sarcastically as

> a mild fellow, gently reared in a middle-sized
> city in Pennsylvania and expensively educated.
> A good-natured child, the older son of civilized
> parents who had quietly died. (Now) a rather
> handsome man of thirty-three. Quieter than
> he once was. A little fussy, perhaps; somewhat
> sententious. Used to getting an answer when
> he spoke politely to someone, and never recon-
> ciled to the brutal manners of the metropolis
> in which (now) he lived. But unresentful. The
> sort of man who doesn't mistreat women, never
> loses his credit cards or breaks a plate while
> washing up, works conscientiously at his job,
> lends money to friends graciously, walks his
> dog each midnight no matter how tired he feels.
> The sort of man it's hard to dislike, and whom
> disaster avoids. (DK, 9)

Of course, disaster will find him aplenty. This advertising-man cipher, who might have stepped out of the pages of Cheever, is going to be plunged into a nightmare, like Edward G. Robinson in Fritz Lang's film noirs. On a train ride to a business conference in a strange city, he will kill a work-man with a crowbar and have sex with a beautiful young blind woman in the bathroom. He will try to confess his crime to the blind woman, who will not believe him. Attempting to make amends for his crime, he will visit the widow of the workman and be so repulsed by her flabby, buxom crudity that he will run fleeing. He will pick up a prosti-tute and have sex with her. He will fall in love with the blind woman and quit his advertising job and establish house with her. They will stay indoors and have sex interminably, become depleted, their relationship go bad. He will wind up in a hospital, on an operating table, and have fevered dreams about coffins (perhaps the killing of the workman was one of them—we're not sure), and die.*

None of it is believable for a second. But then, Sontag is not interested in realism. She shows her

---

* In *The Benefactor*, we and the narrator were led to believe that he has killed his ex-lover. Several chapters later she turns up alive; no harm done. In *Death Kit*, the protagonist struggles to find the proper emotional response to having murdered a workman in a tunnel. He tries to convince oth-ers, who do not believe him. By the book's ambiguous end it appears that he has dreamed the whole killing while under anesthesia, preparatory to an operation that will take his life. In both cases, false alarm, no murder—and no need to feel guilt. Actions do not appear to have consequences, which is good for supporting the notion of a random universe but less good for pulling readers into a novel's plot.

experimental-fiction bona fides by quirks such as double-indented paragraphs, lists, placing the word "now" in parentheses, asking a series of rhetorical questions about motives, switching pronouns from "they" to "we." *Death Kit* is awful, as pretentious as can be. But it does represent an advance over *The Benefactor*, if only because it seems to come from a deeper, more personal place in its author.

The novel, which appeared in 1967, has that grim sensibility of much sixties fiction, satirizing the emptiness of the American dream—a sub-Beckettian outpouring of sour stream-of-consciousness, minus the love Beckett had for his poor bastards. Sontag is eager to show just how hollow, provisional, fake this Diddy is, by assigning him multiple personalities. His attempts to do the right thing are mocked as "Diddy the Good." Later he will be mocked for trying to "use his mind for a change. Make unadulterated contact with the inner man. A task he's been neglecting; for which he's (now) paying the price. Nothing seems to have the right weight any more. He's being light-headed about the serious, solemn about the casual. Diddy the Dunce."

Though mental laziness is despised, obsessive thinking is also portrayed as a dead end. One of Sontag's themes here is the desert of mental entrapment. "He must be here, and not in his head" (DK, 146). Diddy reminds himself, in a be-here-now prod. The point is made even clearer in the final scene, when Diddy realizes, with the sharpness of a mathematical truth: "Life=the world. Death=being completely inside one's head" (DK, 314). The body is life, the mind death—this is a very sixties concept, and worth noting only because it demonstrates an ambivalence that Sontag (whom the media, with her assistance, assigned the role of arch-intellectual) felt at times toward the life of the mind. (In another context she wrote: "the inside of someone's head—that is madness" [WSF, 110].) While it never reached the point of anti-intellectualism, there was this persistent tension in her between love of words (philosophy and literature) and sensual fascination with nonverbal theatre and ritual. In her essay on Canetti, she reversed the mathematical equation by saying that living in one's head could be a hedge against mortality: "So large is the value of the mind that it alone is used to oppose death. Because the mind is so real to him Canetti dares to challenge death, and because the body is so unreal he perceives nothing dismaying about extreme longevity. . . . Rarely has someone been so at home in the mind, with so little ambivalence" (USS, 202–3).

Diddy is one who is not at home in his mind. In *Illness as Metaphor*, there is a curious aside that might well apply to this character: "The passive, affectless anti-hero who dominates contemporary American fiction is a creature of regular routines or unfeeling debauch; not self-destructive but prudent, not moody, dashing, cruel, just dissociated" (IAM, 46).

Death Kit is also a demonstration, if a tedious one, of what she called in another essay, written at the same time as the novel, "states of false (language-clogged) consciousness." In that seminal essay, "The Aesthetics of Silence," Sontag wrote: "Discernible in the fictions of Stein, Burroughs, and Beckett is the subliminal idea that it might be possible to out-talk language, to talk it into silence." She put forward in a neutral tone, neither condemning nor approving, the following concept:

> In the end, the radical critique of consciousness (first delineated by the mystical tradition, now administered by unorthodox psychotherapy and high modernist art) always lays the blame on language. Consciousness, experienced as a burden, is conceived of as the memory of all the words that have been said. Krishnamurti claims that we must give up the psychological,

as distinct from factual, memory. Otherwise,
we keep filling up the new with the old, closing
off experience by hooking each experience into
the last. (SRW, 23)

Sontag seems to be flirting here with the tempta-
tion of getting beyond the psychological, that old
bête noir of hers, even if it means relinquishing
language.

I understand that these ideas have a legitimate
provenance in Eastern thought, but ambivalent
talk about "consciousness as a burden" makes me
nervous. Eventually, it must have made Sontag
nervous too: she stopped citing Krishnamurti,
stopped entertaining as a healthy possibility
the notion of abandoning consciousness, and
became more attached to the necessity of holding onto historical memory, which meant that we
cannot let go of the words, we have to hook each
experience into the last.

Shallow America

In *Death Kit*, Sontag evinces no such ambivalence toward America: she simply doesn't like the
place. This second novel of hers is perhaps her
most sustained attempt to describe contempo-

rary American life, and the problem is that she doesn't know it or its people well enough, so it comes off as slumming. There is contempt for the nine-to-fivers and the corporate world, and sociological cartoons about the inhabitants of suburban homes: "Houses that are quiet (now), emptied of father-breadwinner and school-age children. Being cared for and stocked with provisions by mother-wife and her domestics" (DK, 80). Diddy may not condescend to "their pampered well-fed children; equipped with shiny English bicycles that moved on hard tires, tended by garrulous devoted Irish nursemaids, packed off to their weekly piano lessons," but Sontag surely does. On the other side of town, far from the shiny English bicycles, are the prostitutes and shabby sordid lodgings of the workman's widow, who talks like this: "Why, I used to come home from school with my rear end red as fire! . . . Yeah, they could of used me for a bed warmer, that's how red and hot my little fanny was" (DK, 126).

It's always anomalous when a writer of Sontag's intelligence goes crude or smutty. Maybe it springs from impatience, the wish for Rabelaisian bawdiness to cut through the burdens of consciousness. In any case, Sontag seems to have viewed the United States as relentlessly vulgar, and it brought out the vulgar and unsubtle in her. At roughly the same time she was writing *Death Kit*, she responded to a *Partisan Review* questionnaire, reprinted as "What's Happening in America (1966)" in *Styles of Radical Will* (surely the weakest piece in that otherwise distinguished collection), with let-it-rip rhetoric:

> Today's America, with Ronald Reagan the new daddy of California and John Wayne chawing spareribs in the White House, is pretty much the same Yahooland that Mencken was describing. The main difference is that what's happening in America matters so much more in the late 1960s than it did in the 1920s. Then, if one had tough innards, one might jeer, sometimes affectionately, at American barbarism and find American innocence somewhat endearing. Both the barbarism and the innocence are lethal, outsized today. (SRW, 194)

You'll get no argument from me about the danger American imperial power poses to the world, but I do find her bandying about labels like "barbarism" and "innocence" to be somewhat tired, overly broad and beside the point. Similarly, her potted history and cultural analysis sound skimpy.

Having established that America was founded on genocide and slavery, she goes on to state:

> After America was 'won,' it was filled up by new generations of the poor and built up according to the tawdry fantasy of the good life that culturally deprived, uprooted people might have at the beginning of the industrial era. And the country looks it. Foreigners extol the American 'energy,' attributing to it both our unparalleled economic prosperity and the splendid vivacity of our arts and entertainments. But surely this is energy bad at its source and for which we pay too high a price, a hypernatural and humanly disproportionate dynamism that flays everyone's nerves raw. Basically it is the energy of violence, of free-floating resentment and anxiety unleashed by chronic cultural dislocations which must be, for the most part, ferociously sublimated. This energy has mainly been sublimated into crude materialism and acquisitiveness. Into hectic philanthropy. Into benighted moral crusades, the most spectacular of which was Prohibition. Into an awesome talent for uglifying countries and cities. Into the loquacity and torment of a minority of gadflies, artists, prophets, muckrakers, cranks, and nuts. And into self-punishing neuroses. But the naked

violence keeps breaking through, throwing everything into question. (SRW, 195–96)

To me, this is an imbalanced, overgeneralized and unsubstantiated screed by a hanging judge. It ignores too much about the ideals and achievements of immigrant America. I am not sure why the fantasy of the good life need be "tawdry," or why American energy is "hypernatural" or intrinsically "violent," or why a nation built of immigrants should necessarily be condemned to "chronic cultural dislocations," or why our philanthropy should be dismissed as "hectic," or why our valiant gadflies and muckrakers need be doomed to loquacious torment. But I despair of convincing many cultivated readers that America is not some horrible mistake, at a moment when its foreign and domestic policies are so tragically misguided. Suffice to say, I disagree with Sontag's excessively negative assessment of America, and leave it at that.

Sontag's intemperate tone in the above passage might be contextualized by noting that she was understandably angry, writing in the midst of the Vietnam War. Still, she remained consistent in her statements thereafter, explaining how her dislike for her native country's "materialism" drew her toward Europhilia. As she put it in her

2003 Friedenhaus Acceptance Speech, "[T]here have always been American fellow-travelers of the European cultural ideals (one stands here before you), who find in the old arts of Europe correction and a liberation from the strenuous mercantilist biases of American culture" (ATST, 197). To be fair, her espousal of the Bosnian cause led her to a more critical assessment of Western Europe, in its indifference and passivity to preventing violence, and she did once allow herself to comment on Nazism as "a triumphant barbarism that was (need it be said?) entirely generated from within the heart of Europe" (WSF, 287). But always she returned to her initial position:

> If I must describe what Europe means to me as an American, I would start with liberation. Liberation from what passes in America for a culture. The diversity, seriousness, fastidiousness, density of European culture constitute an Archimedean point from which I can, mentally, move the world. I cannot do that from America, from what American culture gives me, as a collection of standards, as a legacy. Hence Europe is essential to me, more essential than America, although all my sojourns in Europe do not make me an expatriate. (WSF, 286)

There is a funny, chagrined personal essay Sontag wrote in 1987, "Pilgrimage," about her California adolescence, when she was in flight from everything American. "I felt I was slumming, in my own life," she writes, trying to drown out the laugh-track of TV sitcoms with "transformative books," such as Thomas Mann's *The Magic Mountain*. She finally brings herself, with a friend, to ring Mann's doorbell, and they have a chat, the irony of which rests on the fact that she is squirming with embarrassment at her immature country, while he is trying so hard to be charmed by it, meanwhile addressing her as a representative of American youth.

> He asked about our studies. Our studies? That was a further embarrassment. I was sure he hadn't the faintest idea what a high school in Southern California was like. Did he know about Drivers' Education (compulsory)? Typing courses? Wouldn't he be surprised by the wrinkled condoms you spotted as you were darting across the lawn for first period. . . . I hoped he would never find out. He had enough to be sad about—Hitler, the destruction of Germany, exile. It was better that he not know how really far he was from Europe. (PIL, 50)

And to be far from Europe, in her view, was to be far from everything intellectually nourishing.

I find it curious how thoroughly Sontag eschewed American intellectual models, especially since there were a glut of notable essayists still on the scene when she made her debut. For instance, Edmund Wilson's brand of biographical criticism, or his omnivorous reading range and cosmopolitan taste for foreign literature, might have inspired her.[*] The postwar era, 1945–1965, had been a golden era of American critical prose: Wilson, Lionel Trilling, Meyer Shapiro, Harold Rosenberg, Clement Greenberg, Leslie Fielder, Philip Rahv, James Agee, Robert Warshow, Manny Farber, Ralph Ellison, Dwight Macdonald, Pauline Kael, Mary McCarthy, James Baldwin, Edwin Denby, Paul Goodman, Alfred Kazin, Irving Howe, Seymour Krim, Arlene Croce; the

---

[*] Apparently they were social acquaintances. In Wilson's diary, *The Sixties*, he reports in 1963 meeting "a handsome girl from California [Susan Sontag] who is one of Roger's new writers," a reference to editor Roger Straus, of Farrar, Straus. By 1968 he is reporting: "I never have much conversation with Susan Sontag. Roger can't quite forgive me because I am not impressed with her. When I talked to her about the movies in the car, she discussed them in her usual pretentious and esoteric way. *Yellow Submarine* should have stuck to one style, it was a mixture of too many, an 'anthology.'" How funny to picture these two great figures awkwardly debating the merits of *Yellow Submarine*!

list could go on. Yet Goodman and Trilling were the only ones of her countrymen she cited with admiration, and she had already pronounced Trilling's relevance passé. She went out of her way to tell her *Paris Review* interviewer that Mary McCarthy was "a writer who'd never mattered to me." Why not? Hadn't McCarthy, for instance, preceded her in writing dispatches from North Vietnam, which Sontag admitted reading in *Trip to Hanoi*? No doubt Sontag resented the comparisons that saw her early on as "the new Mary McCarthy," or as filling some sort of Dark-Lady-of-the-New York-intelligentsia niche previously occupied by McCarthy. Still, Mary McCarthy could be a fascinating writer; her first essay collection, *On the Contrary*, is as provocative and stylish a debut, in its way, as *Against Interpretation*, and her memoir, *Memories of a Catholic Girlhood*, is a classic of American autobiographical literature. But for Sontag, it would seem, she was incurably middlebrow, not a true intellectual in the European mold.*

Interestingly, in that same *Paris Review* interview, Sontag does credit two American con-

---

* In her diary entry marked 9 Dec. 1961, Sontag writes: "Mary McCarthy's grin—grey hair—low-fashion red + blue print suit. Clubwoman gossip. She is The Group. She's nice to her husband."

temporaries as having influenced her: "I think I learned a lot about punctuation and speed from Donald Barthelme, about adjectives and sentence rhythms from Elizabeth Hardwick." The implication I take from this statement is that Barthelme and Hardwick (the Hardwick of *Sleepless Nights*, not the essays) influenced her fiction writing. She was too proud of her fiction writing to waste time speaking to interviewers about the writers who influenced her essays, and perhaps too proud of her essays to address her apprenticeship in that area.

I don't at all fault Sontag for refusing to engage with the work of American essayists and critics; the European thought of Benjamin, Barthes, Cioran, Bernhard, Sebald, et cetera, fired her imagination, and since it did the trick, she need not have looked elsewhere. Also, by not addressing the American critical tradition, she was able to be heard as more of a unique voice, coming out of nowhere, bringing news of a larger, more ample intellectual life. She was better able to fulfill her role as the bridge between Old World and New World cultures. But this refusal to examine home-grown intellectual models is yet another indication of her dismissal of the American mind, which I cannot help regarding as a bit unfair. I also think she was being "ungrateful," if one can use such a word, for failing to acknowledge that all those aforementioned American critics whose works appeared in *Partisan Review*, *Commentary*, *Art News*, the *New Leader*, and other journals paved the way, creating a warm, inviting context for her own cerebral essays to fit snugly into.

The Volcano Lover

▣ In *The Volcano Lover* (1992), she had at last consummated her desire to write a work of fiction with which she and the world could be pleased. No accident that it is an historical novel: the historical record gave her story a grounding in reality such as her first two novels had lacked. She was also able to draw as well on another armature, *That Hamilton Woman*, with Vivian Leigh and Laurence Olivier, and there is considerable overlap between that lively movie classic and the novel that came after. One might read *The Volcano Lover*, in fact, as a learned, encyclopedic deconstruction of *That Hamilton Woman*. The story revolves around a love triangle between the Cavaliere, the British envoy, William Hamilton, stationed in Naples; Emma, a tartish young beauty with whom the middle-aged, fastidious Hamilton becomes infatuated, to the point of marrying; and Lord Nelson, the naval hero who bests Napoleon, and who wins Emma's heart and body.

Sontag gets around not wanting to do a traditional novel of scenes and dialogue by writing mini-essays about the action. Sometimes *The Volcano Lover* feels more like a commentary on a novel than a novel itself, in much the same way that John Ashbery was said to be writing glosses on non-existent poems, and Borges's stories often read like scholarly summaries of longer works. Actually, Sontag doesn't even call *The Volcano Lover* a novel but, self-consciously, a "romance," thereby linking it to nineteenth-century works such as Hawthorne's *The Scarlet Letter* or *The Blithedale Romance*. Sontag draws pragmatically and sensibly on her main strengths as an essayist, and at the same time attaches herself to that modernist lineage of essayistic novelists (Musil, Broch, Proust, to some extent Mann, Bernhard, Kundera, Sebald—Bellow, too, though she never mentions him). She speculates, she comments, she circles. She breaks the reader's desire for unconscious immersion in a story by drawing attention to the novel's artifice, by shifting tenses and prenomial viewpoints, by intruding contemporary anachronisms (PMS, motorcycles) into the nineteenth-century frame. She inserts herself, the author, into a few scenes as a character, while shifting the action to the twentieth century. She playfully introduces historical figures as characters in the action, such as Goethe and William Beckford; she quotes Voltaire, the Marquis de Sade, Samuel Johnson. She aphorizes constantly, and beautifully: it is the main charm of the book. She makes lists like crazy: the list becomes her expansive prose alternative to the aphorism. She uses no quotation marks in the dialogues, which gives them a floaty quality, as though they could just as easily have been thoughts passing through a character's head as spoken words.

As novelists are wont to do, she parcels out fragments of her personality to the different characters. To the Cavaliere she gives her fastidious taste and her talent for hyperactivity; to Catherine (Hamilton's first wife), her fascination with gay men; to Emma, her vitality and seductive charm reflex that enchanted the likes of Roger Straus and other powerful men in the New York literary world; to Nelson, her intrepid courage and drive for conquest. She pretends to sympathize with Emma (by saying that the powerful woman is always blamed for cruelty, et cetera) but the effort shows. I can't help thinking Emma is her version of the various coquettes Sontag fell madly in love with, who broke her intellectual heart. She's really only sympathetic to the Cavaliere—his love of the rarefied, his dignified refusal of boredom, even his coldness and detachment. "But like many who were melancholy as children, he had a great capacity for self-discipline" (VL, 68).

At the core of the Cavaliere's character is his mania for collecting. Walter Benjamin once wrote a splendid essay "Unpacking My Library," about the psychology of the book-collector, and Sontag foreshadowed her treatment of the Cavaliere's collecting habit with a comment she made in her essay on Benjamin: "In collecting, Benjamin experienced what in himself was clever, successful, shrewd, unabashedly passionate. 'Collectors are people with a tactical instinct'—like courtiers" (USS, 121). She builds on these insights with superb elaborations—and indeed, a small book of witty maxims on collecting might be extracted from this novel. Some examples:

> A gratifying symmetry, that collecting most
> things requires money but then the things collected themselves turn into more money. . . .
> The true collector is in the grip not of what is
> collected but of collecting. . . . To collect is to

rescue things, valuable things, from neglect, from oblivion, or simply from the ignoble destiny of being in someone else's collection rather than one's own. . . . There is no such thing as a monogamous collector. Sight is a promiscuous sense. The avid gaze always wants more. . . . The sweet doom of the collector (or tastemaker . . . but tastemakers are usually collectors). . . . Collections unite. Collections isolate. They unite those who love the same thing. (But no one loves the same as I do; enough.) They isolate from those who don't share the same passion. (Alas, almost everyone.) (VP, 22, 24, 25, 71, 29)

Why not say Sontag is writing here, ironically but still feelingly, about her own lonely avidity as a cultivated person of taste, who spent a lifetime learning to discriminate between objects of greater or lesser beauty? Taste could isolate, even—or especially—for Sontag, who took on the tastemaker's mission to educate the reading public about all the good, refined things they were missing.

The Volcano Lover is the story of someone who is content to live in his head among the glorious artifacts of the past, and who is moved, by unexpected carnal passion, into the present, with disastrous consequences—a variation on the

Death in Venice plot. (Mann was Sontag's dominant first influence in fiction, though she later broke with him, or so she thought.) Sontag was also confessing she had come to care more and more about history, the Old World, and less and less about the new, the innovative, which she had previously specialized in explicating.

Another piece of personal experience drawn on in the novel has to do with travel. Sontag had been spending more and more time abroad, in what amounted to controlled expatriations. "Living abroad facilitates treating life as a spectacle—it is one of the reasons that people of means move abroad," she writes in *The Volcano Lover*. But of course, to reduce life to a spectacle has its bad consequences. At one point she tells us "the Cavaliere was feeling rather, well, Voltairean: in an ethnological mood. On his own. A tourist of other people's superstitions" (VL, 49). In her 1984 essay, "Questions of Travel," she wrote: "To speak in the persona of the traveler, a professional (or even amateur) observer, was to speak for civilization; no premodern travelers thought of themselves as the barbarians. Modern travel literature starts when civilization becomes a critical as well as a self-evident notion—that is, when it is no longer so clear who is civilized and who is not" (WSF, 275). By placing her story in the premodern era, Sontag showed, like it or not, nostalgia for a time when Anglo-American civilization felt less guilt-ridden about its claims to superiority. The cozy, decadent lassitude that settles on the Cavaliere's household in Naples may also be seen as Sontag's modernist critique of the "innocents abroad" theme; while the chaos that ensues once the ménage-à-trois is uprooted from Naples, and which results in the ragged trail of multiple endings that occupy the last quarter of the book, may well express the author's own fatigue with incessant voyaging.

The Volcano Lover keeps picking up speed and then bogging down. In the background, always, lurks the volcano and its promise of a catastrophic denouement. "Maybe it is not the destructiveness of the volcano that pleases us most, though everyone loves a conflagration, but its defiance of the law of gravity to which every inorganic mass is subject. . . . That is why we love trees. Perhaps we attend to the volcano for its elevation, like ballet" (vl, 32). We are equidistant between Sontag's dance writings and her essay on apocalyptic science fiction films. Still, the volcano does not erupt.

What scenes there are have the quality of *tableaux vivants*, rather like those in Kubrick's film *Barry Lyndon*. We are privy to the inner life of all the characters, even the monkey, Jack.* Thankfully, the source material is sufficiently tawdry and melodramatic to overcome Sontag's tendency toward the still life, and keep us impatient to know what happens next.

The great achievement of this novel is its worldliness. Its chief weakness is that is still feels labored, willed. Sontag was not a natural novelist, but she finessed her limitations superlatively this one time, with research, entertaining digressions, and a sensational-tabloid plot.

Performance, Character, and Theatre

🗆 Sontag never created memorable, rounded characters in her fiction. Perhaps it's because she was so fixated on the instability of character, on everyone acting out in rather shallow fashion a succession of roles, that she never could convey a deeper core of self. Proust, too, believed that

---

*"But often when he listened to music—he clearly liked music—he bit his nails; perhaps music made him nervous too. He yawned, he masturbated, he searched for lice in his tail. Sometimes he just paced, or sat staring at the Cavaliere. Perhaps he was bored. The Cavaliere was never bored" (VL, 79).

none of us possess unitary consciousness and that we choose a succession of selves throughout a lifetime, but somehow he managed to bestow on each of his characters a nugget of recognizable, unchangeable being. The hero of *The Benefactor* dissolves into a dream-self that becomes completely malleable. Diddy is presented—and mocked—as a sequence of hypothetical postures (the Good-Bad-Indifferent). Maryna, the heroine of her final novel, *In America*, abandons the Polish stage where she had reigned and emigrates to America, where she plays at communal farming like Marie Antoinette being a shepherdess.

Sontag's main subject as a fiction writer was inauthenticity of feeling—not a bad subject, since nonfeeling is a major trope of modern literature. But Sontag had a hard time making readers care about her particular numbed-out characters. Her watery idea of character meant that she could never succeed as a fiction writer, except in *The Volcano Lover*, where Nelson is a readymade military hero, and the Cavaliere a successful diplomat, and Emma an archetypal femme fatale. But *In America* picks up again the theme of *Death Kit*, that the "I" is a succession of masks and provisional postures. "In almost every case, our manner of appearing *is* our manner of being. The mask is the face," she had written as far back as in "On Style" (AI, 18).

▣ Sontag was a woman of the theatre. One of her finest essays is about the relationship between theatre and film, where she in essence defends the influence of the former on the latter, breaking ranks with "pure cinema." Her one play, the 1993 *Alice In Bed*, is another grim *jeu d'esprit*, but it has its quirky, affecting moments. Emily Dickinson, Margaret Fuller, Kundry from Wagner's *Parsifal*, and the Queen of the Wilis from *Giselle* gather for a tea party around the invalid Alice James, sister of Henry and William. Sontag permits herself a wicked send-up of Henry James's fastidious long-windedness and condescension toward his sister. The dramatic fantasy, in eight scenes, bears some resemblance to the dream plays of Maria Irene Fornes, who had been close to Sontag in the sixties. *Alice in Bed* was, she wrote in the afterword, about the way women silence their creative gifts, "For the obligation to be physically attractive and patient and nurturing and docile and sensitive and deferential to fathers (to brothers, to husbands) contradicts and *must* collide with the egocentricity and aggressiveness and the indifference to self that a large creative gift requires in order to flourish. . . . A play, then, about the grief and anger of women; and finally, a play about the imagination" (AIB, 113, 117).

In America (2000) is all about theatrical folk, a group who always elicited in her warm feelings of substitute family. Actors were given considerable leeway by Sontag, who was as charmed by their egocentric childishness as by their courage in facing audiences and their team solidarity. (See her essay, "Waiting for Godot in Sarajevo," published in *Where the Stress Falls*). Again, in this last novel, she takes up the question of what sacrifices a woman of genius will have to make to fit into ordinary life as wife, mother, communitarian. The novel, however, never comes to a boil, maybe because she had little to say about the theatrical milieu except that she liked it and found it a haven in a hostile world. As always, she was fascinated with divas, but her heroine, Maryna Zalezowska, "Poland's greatest actress," is too sanguine, too sedate a character to inspire genuine conflict. The result is as intelligently written a novel as it is possible to write without its ever coming alive.

The journey of this nineteenth-century Polish theatre troupe though America gives Sontag a pretext to comment on her native country with borrowed distance, like a visitor from a small planet. But she has nothing to say except the usual clichés: that Americans are obsessed with scale, have no true culture, take the pursuit of happiness very seriously, live for money. On the plus side, the setting allowed her to write affectionately about her native California landscape.

The theme of casting about for an identity, a role to fill, ran all through her fiction and most likely her life as well. Tellingly, she wrote in an early diary entry: "Alone, alone, alone. A ventriloquist's dummy without a ventriloquist." So all of us have felt at times, but she was able to circumvent the feeling by turning "Susan Sontag" into a starring public role. In playing it, she resisted pledging allegiance to any pre-established identity, be it American, Jew, or avowed sexual preference. (How hard she made it for interviewers to pin down her precise degree of bisexuality!) By not advancing under any colors other than her own, she could take up more solidly a moral platform, and speak out in the way she most preferred, as an independent moralist. Not that she was incapable of following a party line; theatrical in her presentation of self, she was always casting about for new, juicy roles to fill. Sometimes she seems merely, or too manifestly, to be playing out a role, like the Che Guevara follower in her Cuban Posters essay, or the French intellectual, American style.

She was fascinated with performance—in dance, theatre, film. She herself must have felt awkward or inauthentic at times, locked into the diva role of "Susan Sontag," knowing the distance she had come from Susie Rosenblatt of California, who went to North Hollywood High School. (She took the name of her stepfather, Nathan Sontag, as a teenager.)

In sum she did not create memorable fictional characters. She succeeded so much better at vivid character portraiture in her biographical essays (on Pavese, Benjamin, Canetti, Barthes, Goodman, Artaud, Riefenstahl). Then again, she did create one unforgettable character on the page—the essayist Susan Sontag.

The Essay Form, Transgression, and Innovation

▣ The crisis that Sontag saw in the modern novel—the loss of authority that arose from the death of God and eventually spread to the death of author—she never extended to the essay. That is, she never seemed to doubt her right to put forth her thoughts via a unified, coherent narrative voice in either impersonal or personal essays, without ever raising such self-reflexive specters as the death of the author, the unstable fluid self, the mass media's conditioning mechanisms challenging our very notion of the individual, et cetera. Certainly, she wrote eloquently about the breakdown of authority that had undermined large philosophical treatises, and the recourse of modernist thinkers to fragment, notebook, and aphorism, just as she herself experimented with catchments of notes, quotes, fragments, abecedaries, letters, dialogues, prose-poems, and other formal arrangements in her essays. But she took a quite traditional approach, on the whole, to essayistic discourse. Even in her most splintered essays, she employed a powerful synthesizing voice that oriented the reader like a tuning-fork to an unfolding persuasive argument, and that contributed, from essay to essay, to the multidimensionality of that one truly vivid character she created from scratch, the speaker of her essays.

The fact that she was essentially traditional in her approach to essay voice seems to have led some critics since her death to question her literary importance. In Eliot Weinberger's shrewd if sometimes unfair assessment of Sontag (charging, for instance, that she was too Eurocentric to care about Asian culture, which is certainly untrue) in the *New York Review of Books*, he says that "she never attempted to do anything new or different, formally, with her critical prose. She did not, or could not, follow another Benjamin dictum she cited: 'All great works of literature found a genre or dissolve one.' She was a celebrant of transgression, but there was nothing transgressive about her writing." For this reason Weinberger, himself an experimental writer, concludes, I think quite wrongly, that "she may ultimately belong more to literary history than to literature."

The premise that art must be "transgressive," formally or otherwise, for it to matter seems to me awfully limited, a piece of ideological fashion that will sound like nonsense a hundred years from now. Nothing could be less dangerous or more careerist in academia today than the defense of the "transgressive." No doubt Sontag has much to answer for, in having smoothed the way for the "transgressive" and "subversive" standard, by arguing that the only art that mattered was that which shook up the status quo—an enthusiastic distortion that she rued in retrospect.

Beyond that, there are many experiments a major, if traditional, essayist like Sontag undertakes in her prose writing on a daily basis, having to do with the sentence-by-sentence construction of structural chains of meaning and association, which may fall outside the restricted set of avant-garde sanctioned experiments. True, she did not write destabilized lyric essays, but so what? Sontag's best ruminations have a power and cohesion that merit countless revisitation, both to savor their insights and to wonder how she did it. If that is not making a contribution to literature, I don't know what is.

Don't Get Personal

▣ In her fourth essay collection, *Where the Stress Falls*, a theme began breaking in, almost obsessively: a dislike of the personal in art, and a reverence for the impersonal. She approved the Polish poet Adam Zagajeswki for being "quite at odds with the narcissistic purposes, and pointedly indiscreet contents, of most autobiographical writing," and for not trafficking in "today's cult of the excitements of self" (WSF, 54, 59). Virginia Woolf was commended for saying, "The state of reading consists in the complete elimination of the ego" (WSF, 20). The painter Howard Hodgkins was applauded for portraying "the world that resists and survives the ego," for "what is *not* oneself" (WSF, 156).

Not coincidentally, her opposition to displays of the self in memoir and personal essay dovetailed with her promotion of imaginative fiction above the essay, and her decision to regard herself foremost as a novelist.

> Most people seem to think that writing is just a form of self-regard. Also called self-expression. As we are no longer supposed to be capable of authentically altruistic feelings, we are not supposed to be capable of writing about anyone but ourselves. But that's not true. William Trevor speaks of the boldness of *non*-autobiographical imagination. Why wouldn't you want to escape yourself as much as you might want to express yourself? It is far more interesting to write about others. (WSF, 266)

So she declares with characteristic regal finality—knowing full well that Montaigne, Rousseau, Thoreau, Lamb, and a thousand others did find it more interesting to write about themselves, and enriched literature immeasurably by doing so. A certain amount of autobiographical subjectivity was to be tolerated, provided it turned up in fiction and lyric poetry. Sontag called her first short-story collection *I, etcetera*, mocking the interest one takes in oneself. But notice: she reserved this title for a book of fiction, not essays; some of these stories, such as "Project for a Trip to China," "Debriefing," and "Unguided Tour," were very autobiographical, a license she rarely permitted herself in nonfiction.

The distaste for the personal was in some ways an extension of that earlier distancing of herself from the clumsy inwardness of psychology. In praising Kleist's essay on puppets she writes of his "sublimity of the impersonal . . . as if grace and inwardness were opposed" (WSF, 168–69). She cites Barthes, her exemplar, as moving toward "the great project of depersonalization which is the aesthete's highest gesture of good taste" (WSF, 87). What she found so refreshing in ballet was its "exalted abnegation of the self" (WSF, 196) as exemplified by "Balanchine, who thought ballet should be unconcerned with inner experience" (WSF, 169).

Dance exemplified for Sontag the merger of the spiritual and the impersonal. She quoted Merce Cunningham: "For me, it seems enough that dancing is a spiritual exercise in physical form, and that what is seen is what is" (WSF, 162). Dance also furnished a route to transcending the ego.

> Cunningham is the most important champion
> of the anti-expressive and anti-subjective, and
> the choreographers who studied with him have

extended his emphasis on objectivity. Yvonne Rainer's work in the period of the Judson Dance Theatre aimed at "submerging the personality" in impersonal, task-like movements: "So, ideally, one is not even oneself, one is a neutral doer. . . ." But repetition is also a method for inducing bliss (WSF, 169, 174),

wrote Sontag, the ex–Comparative Religions professor. In the sixties, she had spoken favorably of Eastern religions (she found young people promising, among other reasons, because of "the homage they pay to Oriental thought and rituals" [SRW, 199]), and had been drawn to performance art that achieved a mystical emptying-out approaching silence.

This notion was stated as early as her essay on Bresson in *Against Interpretation*:

The spiritual style of Bresson's heroes is one variety or other of unself-consciousness. (Hence the role of the project in Bresson's films: it absorbs the energies that would otherwise be spent on the self. It effaces personality, in the sense of personality as what is idiosyncratic in each human being, the limit inside which we are locked.) Consciousness of self is the "gravity" that burdens the spirit; the surpassing of the consciousness of self is "grace," or spiritual lightness. (AI, 193).

There is much truth here, even if Bresson's non-professionals fascinate as much because of their idiosyncratic physical features and ways of moving as because of their lack of self-consciousness.

The irony is that she could write stunning and delightfully appealing personal essays and autobiographical fragments: "On Paul Goodman"; "Homage to Halliburton"; "Singleness"; "Thirty Years Later" (her introduction to the reissue of *Against Interpretation*); her charming autobiographical sketch "Pilgrimage" about the visit as a teenager to Thomas Mann's house, which appeared in the *New Yorker* (but which she significantly chose not to reprint in her collections—why, too personal?); "Certain Mapplethorpes"; the first thirty pages of *Trip to Hanoi*; the aforementioned stories in *I, etcetera*; as well as the autobiographical passages in *The Volcano Lover* and *In America* (which are the only lively, convincing pages in that long dull novel). In these autobiographical texts, she achieves the proper balance of honesty, vulnerability, modesty, inward reflection, outgoingness, and cultivated mental alertness. I can't help thinking it is a pity she did not write personally more often.

Clearly, I have my own bias in this matter, having written three personal essay collections and anthologized *The Art of the Personal Essay*. Quite simply, I regard autobiographical writing as a distinguished branch of belles lettres going back to the ancients, and it has nothing for which to apologize, if done well. Yes, too many mediocre memoirs get published, but so do too many mediocre imaginative novels and poetry collections, probably in the same dismal proportion to the quality ones. The backlash against memoir and personal writing has as much to do with class snobbery as with upholding literary standards. Formerly, memoirs and autobiographies were only written by generals, retired politicians, famous authors, actresses, cooks in the White House: in short, those with a claim to prior celebrity or proximity to same. Now that the entrance requirements have widened, the cultural gatekeepers hold their noses with distaste, asking, Who are these nobodies? When Sontag writes "I've never fancied the ideology of writing as therapy or self-expression" (WSF, 260), she seems content to distance herself from the unwashed masses of MFA creative-writing students and wannabe-author housewives who attend summer writing conferences. Yet the marketplace reality is that self-expression alone will not get you very far; even mediocre memoirists need a measure of craft and reader seduction to reach the shores of publication. So "self-expression" turns out to be something of a straw man, not a real threat to culture.

Sontag was not alone in pulling up her skirts at the supposed flood of narcissistic memoirs. There were many such "guild" statements by her peers at the time. In a similar manner, as an officer of PEN-America, Sontag memorably registered her opposition to multiculturalism as a possible vehicle for diluting literary standards by saying, "literature is not an equal opportunity employer."

But snobbism and turf-protection alone would not account for her embrace of the impersonal. For one thing, her dislike of the personal corresponded with a turning-away in Continental philosophy from the subject, the claims of the "I," even as, across the Atlantic, Americans were becoming fascinated with personal narratives and identity politics. For another, the elimination of the ego seems to have been a genuinely attractive goal, if not a possibility, for her. The fact that Sontag was egotistical and self-regarding should not be seen as contradicting her desire to extinguish the ego; quite the contrary. In fact, it was perhaps her uneasiness with the ostentatious public figure she had become, this instantly recognizable being, "Susan Sontag," that drove her into the arms of the impersonal.

In her essay "Singleness," she tackles straightforwardly the triangular relationship between the person she is, the books she has written, and the celebrity she has become. "My books aren't me—or all of me," she writes. "And in some ways I am less than them. The better ones are more intelligent, more talented, than I am; anyway, different. The 'I' who writes is a transformation—a specializing and upgrading, according to certain literary goals and loyalties—of the 'I' who lives" (WSF, 259). Unassailably true; though, so far, any writer might say the same. But she goes on: "Sometimes I feel I'm in flight from the books, and the twaddle they generate." She wants to keep beginning, accepting new challenges (as a novelist), because only in that way can she get away from the "twaddle" about her old (essay) work and the typecasting expectations it has generated—and from her disappointment with what she has achieved on the page, compared to her own exalted standards (WSF, 260).

Sontag had gone on record as saying she did not feel happy about her first two novels, *The Benefactor* and *Death Kit*. The essay "Singleness" ends happily with her reporting that "I got to the point—it took almost thirty years—that I was finally able to write a book I really like: *The Volcano Lover*." She was certainly right to have been dissatisfied with her two first novels, and more pleased with her third, but what is strange is that she never said whether she was similarly disappointed with her first three essay collections, or the book-length nonfiction treatises *On Photography* and *Illness as Metaphor*, and if so, why. It is as though only the fiction counted in her self-assessment.

For her to have written more personally about herself, she might have had to reevaluate her stake in the essays, and be willing to reinvest in and open up the "Susan Sontag" voice-character who spoke them.

For a more personal glimpse, we must look to her diaries, which are scheduled to be published over the next decade. Regardless of whether or not she explicitly gave permission to have them published, the fact remains that she did not live to oversee them into print: to what degree they might represent an inadvertent confession, violating her sense of privacy and wish to avoid autobiography, or the opposite, a long-withheld desire to come clean, to have the last word about herself, we may never know. In any case, the previewed excerpts that have been published already convey the rapid style of these entries, and tell us many revealing things about Sontag, which we might or might not have guessed. For instance, that she was much more filled with self-doubt and uncertainty than she let on, that she imitated the assertive style of Lillian Hellman, that physical beauty was enormously important to her, that she was close friends with Jasper Johns, and reproached herself for sleeping with friends. She rejoices in attaining orgasm, and expresses frank ambivalence about her love of women: "My desire to write is connected with my homosexuality. I need the identity as a weapon, to match the weapon that society has against me. It doesn't justify my homosexuality. But it would give me—I feel—a license. I am just becoming aware of how guilty I feel being queer." Such statements elucidate the tightrope performance of "Notes on Camp."

More startlingly, she declares early on: "The only kind of writer I could be is the kind who exposes himself. . . . To write is to spend oneself, to gamble oneself. But up to now I have not even liked the sound of my name. The writer is in love with himself . . . and makes his books out of that meeting and that violence." Knowing that she began in such a different place, her recoil from the personal makes more sense.

Later Memories of Sontag

▣ As a young woman, especially, Sontag was strikingly good-looking, though I never found her exactly beautiful, the way she appeared in her photographs. She always seemed to me at odds with herself, like a female *luftmensch*, a Jewish-scholar-type coming late to sensuality. Perhaps, too, I could never allow myself to be that physically attracted to her because I feared her quickness to dismissal. But I did admire that Sontag was full of life. She had amazing stores of animal vitality, and I think this vitality was the key to what made her feel superior to others, even more than her intelligence. She had a hearty presence in social situations—hearty or impatient, one or the other. The impatience, it seemed to me, was to find the moment when she could release her presentational daemon. That was the theatrical side of her, like actors who idle in neutral gear, irritable, until they can go onstage or before the camera.

Later, when she became an icon, sitting for a Warhol screen test, doing a cameo in Woody Allen's *Zelig*, or serving as the punchline of *New Yorker* cartoons and *Gremlin 2* jokes (the invading creatures' spokesman explains, "We want civilization: Chamber music . . . the Geneva convention accord . . . Susan Sontag"), and she had that white skunk-streak in her hair that made her even more instantly recognizable, she would do this maddening stunt at film screenings: she would come to the first row before the movie started and stroll along the apron of the stage so that everyone could see she was in attendance, and her eyes might rove impatiently over the audience, seeing but not locking eyes with anyone in particular. Those who knew her, friends or acquaintances, would call out "Susan! Susan!" and she refused to acknowledge any of them, to engage these importuning nobodies' (or so they were left feeling) eye contact. In this way she made herself visually available and yet inaccessible.

🔲 Another memory: one time I was visiting Dan Talbot, the art-house owner and New Yorker film distributor, to pick up a 16mm print he was letting me borrow for my film history class at a local elementary school, P.S. 75, and Sontag happened to be in his office. Dan was about to open Sontag's documentary, *Promised Lands*, about the Israeli-Palestinian conflict, and she was there to go over final details. "How do you want to be described, Susan?" asked Dan. "The publicity people need an answer." She thought for about fifteen seconds and tossed out "International Jew." It seemed a surprising ad lib, especially since she had just made a film that took issue with the official position of the Israeli government. Sontag and Talbot invited me to the press screening the following week.

I arrived at the screening room on time, but the projection was delayed because Sontag, nervously patrolling the entrance, was waiting for Alex Lieberman to show up. Lieberman, the powerful Conde Nast art director and painter, was also a New York internationally pedigreed social lion of the sort Sontag cared most to impress. Finally he arrived, and the screening was allowed to start. Leisurely long-shots of Arab shepherds on a hill alternated with talking heads of various pundits; it was actually a creative solution to the usual documentary style—you sensed her trying to bring an abstract Straub-Huillet approach to this explosive topic. I found myself engaged and engrossed, thinking it was looking like her best film by far. The complex reality of the Middle East conflict had given her a way out of the erotic archness that ruined her debut film, *Duet for Cannibals*, or the spiritual archness that undercut her second feature, *Brother Karl*. The problem was that because of Lieberman's tardiness the screening would now run about twenty minutes late, which would make me twenty minutes late for my rendezvous with my then-girlfriend Liz a few subway stops away: she would be getting off from work, we were set to go out to dinner, we had recently patched up a fight, and she would not like to be kept standing on a street corner; beside which I am fiercely punctual, hating to make anyone wait for me. So, regretfully, I got up and left the theatre ten or fifteen minutes from the end, as unobtrusively as possible. The director was pacing outside the doors, and when she saw me attempting to make my discreet exit, called out, "You have to see the last ten minutes! It's the most powerful scene in the film." "I'm sure it is, Susan, but I'm going to have to see it some other time, because I'll be late for an appointment—" "You have to go back, it makes no sense without the end," she called after me, to no avail. How had I risen in importance so suddenly that my opinion mattered one way or the other? It was not I personally, the ex-Columbia student now freelance writer who mattered, I realized, but my back—that is, I mattered by virtue of my symbolic capacity as the world's representative to walk out on her, rejecting her creative effort.

I seemed to have a knack for such disappointing exits in her presence. One time I noticed that there was a single screening of Hans-Jurgen

Syberberg's newest film, *Die Nacht* (*The Night*), at the Anthology Film Archives, which was then in the New York Shakespeare Building on Astor Place. The film, the ad in the *Village Voice* said, would be starring "the great European actress Edith Clever." I had seen Clever only in the title role of Rohmer's *The Marquise of O*, but she had certainly acquitted herself well in that part, so I was curious to see her in this performance. The audience was not large, but it included Susan Sontag and her editor-friend Sharon Delano. Sontag, clearly proprietary about Syberberg in America, and a connoisseur of diva actresses from Sarah Bernhardt to the present, approved of my catching this rare experience "for the happy few," as it were. I was not put off by its being essentially a filmed document of a theatrical piece, nor was I bothered by the fact that it was a solo performance, but I was disturbed that the whole thing was in German (a language I do not speak) without subtitles—I could not make heads or tails of anything going on—and it was scheduled to last five hours! At the intermission I got up, never to return.

▣ When I was teaching in the University of Houston's writing program, Susan Sontag came down twice as our visitor. The first time was as part of a general conference to promote PEN-Southwest, the local chapter of PEN-American Center, and the parent chapter located in Manhattan sent down a bunch of distinguished writers, Sontag among them, to read and speak on panels. Sontag was a big wheel in PEN-American Center, as was Donald Barthelme, who taught on our faculty; he was always suggesting we bring Susan down, as he thought very highly of her (and she even more highly of him—she was in awe of him, for he was her model of the literary modernist). On the panel she seemed cross, impatient, and eager to pick a fight, irritably chastising American fiction writers of today for betraying the avant-garde ideals of high modernism. Her position was perfectly legitimate, but I had heard it a dozen times before and so was a little impatient myself with her schoolmarmish scolding of the audience for misguided attachment to realism. I also felt she was showing her loyalty to Donald Barthelme in his "house," a touching gesture, in retrospect

Later that night there was a party, and Hans Magnus Enzensberger, the German writer, was the guest of honor. Donald went around introducing people to "Hans Magnus," a name he seemed to love pronouncing, in his ironic baritone, urging wine refills on everyone with a gracious, seigniorial manner (think Burt Lancaster's Count in *The Leopard*). Sontag was noticeably more relaxed in the company of Enzensberger, an international A-list eminence, than she had been earlier with the Houston notables or her fellow road-show writers.

A few years later, as part of the Houston Reading Series, she came down to give a reading and talk to our graduate students. The series was meant to be a prestigious event, with only five reading slots a year, held in the Museum of Fine Arts auditorium designed by Mies van der Rohe. Having Sontag participate in the series was certainly a feather in our cap—and if not quite an honor for her, at least a decent paycheck. She was to spend two or three days in town. I had arranged for one of our graduate fiction-writing students, a woman who had already earned a doctorate in literature and was fluent in French and had read every one of Sontag's books, to pick her up at the airport.

Susan seemed testy when I came by for her later that night. "Why did you get that little housewife to drive me around?" she said.

I could only laugh: this was la Sontag, when she unhappily found herself outside New York, Paris, or Berlin. An eager, practiced world traveler, ostensibly open to all new experience, she was nevertheless infamously rude to her academic hosts, doing her best imitation of Bette Davis in *Beyond the Forest* ("What a dump!"), when passing through what she regarded as the American provinces. People I knew used to get together and top each other with stories about how impossible Sontag had been when she visited their campus. Such anecdotes proliferate in the book by Carl Rollyson and Lisa Paddock, *Susan Sontag: The Making of an Icon*, or in Terry Castle's or Camille Paglia's first-person testimonies. We do not have to rehearse them again, as they all boil down to the same story: Sontag is condescending, curt, and demanding toward those she regards as minions. She arrives late, insults the audience, and gives a perfunctory performance. It does not take much insight to see underneath this contempt a large sense of insecurity at being, herself, an *arriviste* in the great world. She did not have that natural-aristocratic manner that, for instance, Barthelme displayed, which knew how to put servants and functionaries at ease; she was made of socially coarser stuff. I must say that, up to a point, her rudeness never bothered me. I was amused by that impossible side of her (so reminiscent of my actress-mother) and a part of me sympathized with it, having come myself from an even lower, less polished social background than she had.

But I also sympathized with those left quaking by her. The misunderstandings that ensued could invariably be traced to the same mistake she made over and over: underestimating the intelligence of others. Once she was at the New York City Ballet watching Balanchine's *Bugaku*, a highly exotic, erotic ballet, and she turned to her companion Bob Garels and said, "We are probably the only two people in this audience who realize it's all about *sex*." Well, no: most Balanchine lovers perceived the strong sensual undertow in his ballets, and *Bugaku* is explicitly sexual. Again, when she visited the University of Houston and spoke to my graduate students, she berated them for wanting to become writers when they were so ill-read. "What have you been reading?" she challenged them, and they, polite Southwestern kids for the most part, remained silent, as little apt to brag about their bookishness as Navajo schoolchildren would be to yell out the correct answers and embarrass fellow classmates. "You see?" she said triumphantly, her suspicions confirmed, "You're not reading enough." Okay, maybe no one is reading enough. But I knew, because I had assigned the syllabus, that many of them were in fact reading Balzac's *Lost Illusions*, Walter Benjamin's study of Baudelaire, Goethe's *Italian Journey*, Andre Biely's *St. Petersburg*, Tanizaki's *The Makioka Sisters* and other works that were right up Sontag's alley. She would never discover that because she had already made up her mind that they were poorly read.

Sontag seemed tense when she arrived in Houston that second visit, and I later discovered it was because she expected to be attacked. Not long before, she had criticized the American Left for failing to be honest enough about the horrors of Stalinism, and had issued her aphoristic mot, "communism is Fascism with a human face." She had indeed taken some flack in the leftwing press for equating communism with fascism, and for seeming to renege on earlier, revolutionary-socialist sympathies. The point is that she expected to be heckled for her provocative political stance, and she even referred to that controversy in her opening remarks, but of course no one in Houston knew what she was talking about, or if a handful did, they were certainly too Southern-polite ever to embarrass a distinguished visitor by attacking her in public! If anything, Houston high society—those who went to the opera, the ballet, museum openings, and our Reading Series—was obsessed with the British royals. A visit from Princess Margaret had generated far more excitement than any Left-sectarian debate ever could. But Sontag, coming from the rough-and-tumble of New York literary life, felt vulnerable to ideological attack, and I actually think she was disappointed when none occurred.

Before her reading, I took Sontag out to dinner with Karl Kilian, a cultured man-about-town who owned and ran the Brazos Bookstore, then the unofficial heart of Houston's cultural life. Surrounded by two men, she was flirtatious, and even said at one point: "Phillip, find me a man."

"But Susan," I stuttered tactlessly, "I thought you were, er—"

"Oh, no. It's just there are no good men available."

It was at that dinner before her reading that I reminded her of the group of literary undergraduates to which I had belonged (some of whom she had invited to take part in her downtown writing group), and she acknowledged, "Yes, you were the only one who made it," more or less as I hoped she would. Not that it changed anything between us.

She had had a fair amount of wine to drink, which might not have been such a good thing. When she arrived at the museum auditorium, and looked around at the packed, adoring house,

I sensed her body tense against that Houston crowd. She could really charm an audience or the opposite. That night, it was the opposite. She announced that she was going to read a story they would probably dislike (the implication being that it would be too cerebral for them, or not pandering enough), and proceeded to read it in such a dour, punishing way, that her warning became a self-fulfilling prophecy.

The next day, I met with Sontag to interview her, at the request of Karl Kilian, who thought it would be useful "for the archives." I brought a portable tape recorder with me. Sontag was in good spirits, and warm toward me personally, as if acknowledging that in a strange city where she felt ill-at-ease and knew very few people, I was at least a familiar face, someone on her wave-length. We talked at first about movies, since it was a love we both shared, then about people we knew in common, then about the past, her past. All this while I had the tape recorder turned off. It was then that she began speaking fondly, to my surprise, about her ex-husband Philip Rieff. The tenderness with which she recalled those days of love and early marriage was so open and forthcoming that I felt we, too, could have talked for hours.

But I needed something for posterity, so I turned on the tape. Instantly she froze. It was striking the way she turned into a rigidly defensive public figure, who may as well have been a politician, so wary was she of being misquoted. I tried to get her talking about essay writing, but found her resistant. At that moment I was in the midst of planning my anthology, *The Art of the Personal Essay*, I was besotted and saturated with the form, and here was someone who practiced it on such a high level, someone I respected as much as any essayist alive. She could not have been more bored. It was as though I were insulting her innermost core by asking about her essays instead of her fiction. I tried to get her onto the subject of aphorisms, and Ralph Waldo Emerson, knowing how she loved him, as did I. Her responses were brusque: "Well, of course, Emerson. What is there to say? Aphorisms, yes, we love them." It was a disaster. I ended up not being able to use any of the interview.

(Years later the poet Ed Hirsch, who had successfully interviewed her, told me that it had taken him quite awhile—days, in fact—to get her to unclench and trust the interview process and the tape recorder. I came to see that dramatic shift from sweet and outgoing to guarded and angry as characteristically Sontagian.)

Before we parted in Houston, I gave her a signed copy of my most recent book, it may have been either *Bachelorhood* (my first personal essay collection) or *The Rug Merchant* (a novel). It was all right to give her the book, but then I expressed the wistful hope that she read it. It was an awkward thing for me to me to have said, and it came from that old wish that she would finally take in my literary merits, recognize me, if not as a peer then as a fellow-practitioner. She immediately crushed that idea by replying, affronted, "I read everything in my library." In other words, rather than acknowledge in human terms my vulnerability regarding her opinion, which lay behind my gauchely expressed wish, she took it as an accusation on my part that she was a slacker, which of course no one could ever reasonably accuse Susan Sontag of being.

I was reminded of this moment some time later, when I read an adoring profile of her in the *Sunday Times Magazine*, which featured a photograph of the wall of books in her Manhattan apartment, and quoted her as saying "I've read all these books" or something to that effect. Well, I thought, no one who owns thousands of books has read *all* of them, since there are bound to be reference books, encyclopedias, glossaries, and atlases, and other new books and galleys sitting in piles that people have sent you which you haven't merged yet into the system—and in general, if you're a book collector, you're likely to stockpile some for a rainy day. I know I do—at least a quarter of my library is still waiting to be read. But it was more important for Sontag to boast to the journalist that she had read everything in her library than to state what I assumed to be the more modest truth. Or maybe she *was* being truthful, and I just couldn't credit the veracity of her claim because it lay so far out of my experience.

🗇 Over the years, whenever I would read an essay of hers praising some writer or filmmaker I loved, I would think, "My God, we have so many tastes in common! We both care about the same things! Wouldn't it be nice if we could be friends?" I would fantasize having our dinners around town or dropping in at her apartment and comparing notes on the latest cultural doings. But of course any friendship would have had to be predicated on mutual respect, since I could never bring myself to play the flunky. On my end, I would also have to surrender some of my own judgmental wariness about her and trust her more. Above all, you look into the eyes of an acquaintance and see permission to take it further, or not; I never saw that permission in Sontag's eyes. I don't think she was even looking for it in my eyes. So a friendship between us never came to pass.* We would get as far as to exchange phone numbers, then neither of us would call the other.

But we kept running into each other. In the 1980s, when AIDS was cutting a fatal path through the New York arts community, several times Susan and I spoke at the same memorial service for a mutual friend. I remember Susan talking quite a bit about Susan at those memorials; but then, I was sometimes guilty of the same. Is it the nature of memorial speakers to be competitive with each other, or is it just me? I always tried to be funnier and more touching in my remarks than she was, and meanwhile she conveyed the impression of being the main event.

We also encountered each other at the New York Film Festival. During the years when I served as one of the selectors of the New York Film Festival, as she had done previously, she always took a rather severe line toward the present committee, as though we were showing films that might not be adhering to quite as high a stan-

---

* It crossed my mind more than once that I had the same first name as her ex-husband.

dard of cinematic rigor as had the committees on which she served. I remember bumping into her in the street down in Soho, and Sontag telling me that the best film in the festival was a Korean one, *The Man With Three Coffins*, which everyone was ignoring but which I must see. I told her that I also loved the film, had in fact campaigned for it as a committee-member to be in the festival. She seemed thrown off-balance: she wanted to be the one to offer tips on what was cutting-edge, and found it hard to believe anyone else could have beaten her to it.

In the late 1980s, when I was on the New York Film Festival selection committee for the first time, a documentary short was submitted to us about Sarah Bernhardt, directed by Edgardo Cozarinsky and narrated by Sontag (the text had also been written by her). Since Cozarinsky, the Argentinian-Parisian filmmaker, was an artist I much respected, as I did Sontag, I pressed hard for us to include the film in our festival, despite the fact that it was a rather conventional rumination on the Divine Sara and the phenomenon of celebrity divas. We paired it with an effervescently light-comic feature made by a young Italian woman director, set in the eighteenth century. The first night the program showed, it was my job to make introductions of the filmmakers to the public, so I was in the Green Room backstage a half-hour before curtain, when Susan swept in requesting that I find twenty seats for her claque, who were waiting outside. Though I had never heard of so many free passes being demanded, particularly for a short, particularly at the last moment, luckily I was able to accommodate her, with seats on the side boxes where the filmmakers and their guests generally sat and, spotlit afterward, received applause.

Seeing the director of the charming Italian feature film standing a few feet away, I thought to introduce Sontag to her. "Oh, we don't want to stay for that crap!" Susan said in her emphatic voice, which I prayed the Italian woman had not heard. (The Moravia situation all over again.) Whether or not she had ever seen the Italian film before pronouncing it "crap," I was not going to try to argue her out of her dismissal, lest her voice carry to the filmmaker. Even if the poor woman, who it was very likely knew of and esteemed Sontag, had not overheard this severe judgment on the crucial occasion of her New York premiere, she could not fail to be wounded later by twenty audience members in her vicinity leaving before the first image of her film was projected.

That, however, was not Sontag's concern. In a way, I had to admire the consistency of her *chutz-*

pah. The world would be a drabber place without such grandly entitled souls.

For all the rudeness of her sacred-monster persona, I miss her. She took literature seriously, cared about the life of the mind, and made you feel at least that there was a game somewhere, with high stakes. I teach her reflective essays as an exemplary countermodel to the MFA creative nonfiction vogue that tries to do everything in scenes, dialogue, and cinematic detail. Though I no longer fantasize winning her approval, I still think of her as a kindred spirit. How wonderful it would be to get her take on the latest opera production, novels, dance, and movies, and how sad that we can't hear her gruff-voiced opinions anymore!

Let me keep her around a little longer. I am not done with my assessment. There are still weighty matters to consider: photography, politics, illness, greatness.

Writings on Photography

🔲 *On Photography* (1977) grew out of a series of essays for the *New York Review of Books*, and took five years to write. Objectively speaking, it is impressive: Sontag tackled a big subject, the history of photography and its role in the modern world, and synthesized vast amounts of information, making theoretical arguments in a lucid, elegant way. Still, I have always found it disappointing or less than meets the eye: dazzling insights side by side obvious points and dubious assertions, and a prosecutorial style that attempts to put photography in the dock.

What's the harm in taking a picture? Plenty, according to Sontag. The shutterbug snaps pictures out of workaholic "anxiety," and is a "voyeur" and a "supertourist" who tries to control the Other with "imperial" aims, or worse. "There is an aggression implicit in every use of the camera," "a camera is sold as a predatory weapon. . . . The camera/gun does not kill, so the ominous metaphor seems to be all bluff—like a man's fantasy of having a gun, knife, or tool between his legs" (OP, 14). Speaking as a man, I suspect this may be a less common male fantasy than Sontag supposes, but we'll let it stand for now, seeing as she's on a roll: "[j]ust as the camera is a sublimation for a gun, to photograph someone is a sublimated murder—a soft murder, appropriate to a sad, frightened time" (OP, 14–15). Nonsense, but nicely written. Sontag is in the business of pumping out memorable phrases here, like "all photographs testify to time's relentless melt," and she does so with panache. Photography is taken to task both for violating the privacy of its subjects and for inducing a habit of nonintervening passivity in the presence of evil. "The person who intervenes cannot record; the person who is recording cannot intervene" (OP, 12). Actually, most photographers in the field will tell you there were times when they put down their cameras to intervene; every situation is different and subject to the negotiations of conscience. But Sontag does not want to address the fuzzy areas; it's all either/or.

Sontag is being the law-giver: X is Y, Y is merely Z, X is no more than Y and Z. "The knowledge gained through photographs will always be some kind of sentimentalism, whether cynical or humanist" (OP, 24). Her demystification of photography unleashes her aphoristic talent but not her enthusiastic affection or tenderness, and the accumulated scorn wearies.

The curious thing is that Sontag obviously relished photography, but couldn't resist taking a hostile attitude toward it, couldn't allow her love to show through. Her unimpressed manner spoke for high culture's resentment against the medium at a time when it was getting so much new attention in museums and at auction houses, the prices for art photographs steadily mounting. The austere decision not to include any photographs in the book ensured that the focus would remain on her theoretical concerns, even as it rendered them somewhat arid and arbitrary. The book would have been better, would have invited more two-way conversation, had she included images, and had she looked at individual photographs more closely. For someone who put such stress on style in her first book of essays, she pays remarkably little attention to the visual properties of photographs. When she does come to discuss specific photographers in later chapters, she takes a surprisingly narrow, moralistic viewpoint, which causes her to misjudge the range and artistic depth of, say, a Diane Arbus.

Though the book was greeted by American critics as something wholly original, much of it derives from European cultural criticism: Michel Foucault, in its emphasis on power and control as the universal yardstick; Guy Debord (the emptying-out of reality by "spectacle," the image-world replacing the real one, a notion that would be elaborated by Jean Baudrillard as the theory of "simulacra"); the sociological frame–criticism of the *Cahiers du Cinema* group; and, as always, Roland Barthes (who also wrote on photography) and Walter Benjamin, whom Sontag called "photography's most original and important critic," and to whom she would pay touching tribute in her final section, "A Brief Anthology of Quotations [Homage to W. B.]," it having been one of Benjamin's dreams to compose an entire essay out of others' quotes. Still in her Marxist phase, Sontag declared: "The best writing on photography has been by moralists—Marxists or would-be Marxists—hooked on photographs but troubled by the way photography inexorably beautifies." Characteristically, she did not cite any American contemporary photography critics, such as Alan Sekula, A. D. Coleman, or Max Kozloff, who had been plowing the same ground for some time, but instead had to reach back to Paul Rosenfeld's 1924 *Port of New York* to find another trustworthy countryman.

Having subjected the medium to a thoroughly disenchanted analysis in her first chapter ("In Plato's Cave"), she then went on in chapter 2 ("America, Seen Through Photographs, Darkly") to extend her critique to the United States and its representations in photography. I regard *On Photography* partly as an extension of Sontag's ongoing attack on the United States and the presumptions of humanism: for imperial tourist, substitute Ugly American. Her argument traces the idea of America from Whitman's democratic vistas through the "pious uplift" of the *echt*-humanist "Family of Man" exhibit curated by Edward Steichen, to the "sour" "anti-humanist" visions of Robert Frank and Diane Arbus. Just as Sontag cleverly finds a way to equate Steichen and Arbus ("both render history and politics irrelevant. One does so by universalizing the human condition, into joy; the other by atomizing it, into horror" [OP, 33]), so she manages to have it both ways, by attacking the "big business and consumerism" of America and, simultaneously, the too-easy, grotesque caricaturing of the country by its contemporary photographers.

Chapter 3, entitled "Melancholy Objects," is largely a restatement (duly credited) of Benjamin's ideas about class tourism, the *flâneur*, and the innate surrealism of photography. She also attempts to apply Benjamin's notion of the "aura" to what's wrong with America: "Fewer and fewer Americans possess objects that have a patina, old furniture, grandparents' pots and pans—the used things, warm with generations of human touch, that Rilke celebrated in *The Duino Elegies* as essential to a human landscape. Instead, we have our paper phantoms, transistorized landscapes. A featherweight paper museum" (OP, 68). Thus, she conflates everything she doesn't like about the transience of the modern world with "America," and blames photographs for holding our memories, as opposed to Gramps' pots and pans.

It is only when she gets to the fourth essay, "The Heroism of Vision," that she settles down, calmly and dispassionately discussing specific photographs. Perhaps her initial focus on the pioneering nineteenth-century photographers in this chapter has allowed her to approach the subject with more respect; she goes on to analyze the competing claims of beauty and truth as manifested in the photographs of Paul Strand, Edward Weston, Jacob Riis, and others. She has excellent things to say: "Insofar as photography does peel away the dry wrappers of habitual seeing, it creates another habit of seeing: both intense and cool, solicitous and detached; charmed by the insignificant detail, addicted to incongruity" (OP, 99).

She is equally astute in the next chapter, when she takes up the problem of a populist medium, available to everyone, which must assert sophisticated, auteurist claims if it is to be regarded as an art form. She talks about the older generation photographers' suspicions of the intellect, their need to

pass through a cloud of unknowing. . . . Cartier-Bresson has likened himself to a Zen archer, who must *become* the target so as to be able to hit it; 'thinking should be done beforehand and afterwards,' he says, 'never while actually taking a photograph.' Thought is regarded as clouding the transparency of the photographer's consciousness, and as infringing on the autonomy of what is being photographed. Determined to prove that photographs could—and when they are good, always do—transcend literalness, many serious photographers have made of photography a noetic paradox. Photography is advanced as a form of knowing without knowing: a way of outwitting the world, instead of making a frontal attack on it. (OP, 116)

It is in such cool, balanced passages, sympathetic to the photographic viewpoint without necessarily submitting to it, that *On Photography* becomes most alive and stimulating.

In her last essay, "The Image-World," Sontag returns to the theme she had stated rather shrilly at the beginning, when she warned that we were becoming "addicted" "image junkies" drowning in "mental pollution." What she cannot forgive photography is its ubiquity. Part of her argument has to do with the consequences of image-overload in photographs depicting suffering. After World War II, the first photographs from the Nazi death camps had great impact—certainly on her as a teenager, she reports. But, she insists, repeated viewings of "'concerned' photography has done at least as much to deaden conscience as to arouse it. . . . The same law holds for evil as for pornography. The shock of photographed atrocities wears off with repeated viewings, just as the surprise and bemusement felt the first time one sees a pornographic movie wear off after one sees a few more." I don't agree: I don't think photographed atrocities are analogous to pornography, and for that reason they carry an additional impact, making our stomachs flip-flop or our eyes turn away in haste each time we see them. Still, the accusatory sweep of Sontag's prose bears us ever forward, whatever objections silently register. In the end she calls for an "ecology not only of real things but of images as well" (OP, 180). As with her earlier demand for "an erotics of art," it is hard to imagine exactly how one would put this sweeping prescription into effect. An "ecology of images"? Easier said than done.

In her second book on photography, *Regarding the Pain of Others*, which appeared in 2003, some twenty-six years after the first, Sontag takes issue with many of the points she made in *On Photography*. Some of her self-rebutting comments are delightfully frank in puncturing her own earlier bombast. For instance: "There isn't going to be an ecology of images. No Committee of Guardians is going to ration horror, to keep fresh its ability to shock" (RPO, 108). Or:

> In the first of the six essays in *On Photography* (1977), I argued that while an event known through photographs certainly becomes more real than it would have been had one never seen the photographs, after repeated exposure it becomes less real. As much as they create sympathy, I wrote, photographs shrivel sympathy. Is this true? I thought it was when I wrote it. I'm not so sure now. What is the evidence that photographs have a diminishing impact, that our culture of spectatorship neutralizes the moral force of photographs of atrocities? (TPO, 105)

What, indeed? Now she is even willing to challenge the theories of Guy Debord and Jean Baudrillard, "who claims to believe that images, simulated realities, are all that exist now; it seems to be something of a French specialty. . . . To speak of reality becoming a spectacle is a breathtaking provincialism" (RPO, 109–10).

Undoubtedly, it was her own exposure to war in Sarajevo that gave her the experience to rethink her earlier positions, and to champion common sense against the fancy rhetoric of theoreticians who had not been battle-tested. She knew now that victims under fire, such as the Bosnians, wanted to be photographed, to have their sufferings reach the eyes of the world. She knew also that she lacked definitive answers about the effects that war photography might have, for good or ill. She was less inclined to put dubious, ironic quotes around terms like concerned photography. *Regarding the Pain of Others* is altogether a more measured, sober, qualifying, and open-ended book. It proceeds by asking a series of questions about the nature of empathy, the difference between acknowledging and protesting suffering, the appetite for pictures which show bodies in pain, the iconographic tradition such pictures draw on (a helpful digression that takes us through Titian, Callot, and Goya). The prose style is simpler, less opaque, less beautiful, less preening than in *On Photography*, and inclined to break into sentence fragments. "Photographs of an atrocity may give rise to opposing responses. A call for peace. A cry for revenge. Or simply the bemused awareness, continually restocked by photographic information, that terrible things happen" (RPO, 13). This is the prose manner of late Sontag: forthright, conversational, much-interviewed, and, hearing that interviewee voice in her head, transcribing it straight out.

She still showed on occasion a prosecutorial tendency to think the worst of photographers' motives. Thus, she accused the Crimean War photographer Roger Fenton of staging his famous shot of cannonballs strewn on the road: "After reaching the much-shelled valley approaching Sebastopol in his horse-drawn darkroom, Fenton made two exposures from the same tripod position: in the first version . . . the cannonballs are thick on the ground to the left of the road, but before taking the second picture—the one that is always reproduced—he oversaw the scattering of cannonballs on the road itself" (RPO, 53–54).

The filmmaker Errol Morris has questioned this assertion, since there was no proof that Fenton had gone to the trouble of scattering cannonballs, and since the order of the photographs might just as plausibly have been reversed. The obsessive Morris went to considerable trouble to ascertain the order of the two photographs from visual evidence of shadows and angles, even journeying to the site in the Crimea, and concluded Sontag was right that the cannonballs-on-the-road shot was taken after the empty road shot, but that it was still impossible to decide whether the shot was posed by Fenton. "The minute we start to conjecture about Fenton's reasons, his intent—his psychological state—we are walking on unhallowed ground," wrote Morris in his *New York Times* blog.

In the process, Morris also tracked down the man who had initially given Sontag the idea that Fenton had staged the shot, Mark Haworth-Booth, former curator of photography at the Victoria and Albert Museum, who explained:

> Mark Holborn, Sontag's editor in London, called me and told me that Sontag was looking for material about Fenton, and I sent him some photocopies of a thing I'd written a long time ago. He passed them on to her, and she was very grateful. She didn't really quote them accurately. She overstated what I said, which was very characteristic of her writing. I was raising doubts, but she assumed that my doubts were a matter of fact rather than speculation. (Morris, *New York Times* blog)

Sontag's rush to assert that many war photographs had been staged bespoke her old animus against realism, and, in her words, "the presumption of veracity." It also seemed to grow out of her own experiences under fire in Sarajevo, which inclined her to disparage the physical prudence of others. She had gone from an earlier detestation of everything military to a somewhat macho pride in having survived a war zone. Terry Castle's mischievous memoir-piece about Sontag in the *London Review of Books* (17 March 2005) describes this side of her:

> She'd been telling me about the siege and how a Yugoslav woman she had taken shelter with had asked for her autograph, even as the bombs fell around them. She relished the woman's obvious intelligence ('Of course, Terry, she'd read *The Volcano Lover*, and like all Europeans, admired it tremendously') and her own sangfroid. Then she stopped abruptly and asked, grim-faced, if I'd ever had to evade sniper fire. I said, no, unfortunately not. Lickety-split she was off— dashing in a feverish crouch from one boutique doorway to the next, white tennis shoes a blur, all the way down the street to Restoration Hardware and the Baskin-Robbins store. Five or six perplexed Palo Altans stopped to watch as she bobbed zanily in and out, ducking her head, pointing at imaginary gunmen on rooftops and gesticulating wildly at me to follow.

There is a long tradition of American writers testing their nerve by contact with the battleground, but most of them have been men. The only established writer I can think of to have done so in our day is Susan Sontag, who was fully aware of the irony that it took a woman to show such bravery. Her experiences abroad as a witness to war also gave more credibility to the outrage expressed in her last essay on photography, "Regarding the Torture of Others," about Abu Ghraib.

Taking a leaf from Orwell's "Politics and the English Language," she analyzes the Bush administration's employment of linguistic euphemism and evasion about the systematic use of torture. "Apparently it took the photographs to get their attention, when it became clear that they could not be suppressed; it was the photographs that made all this 'real' to them." While deploring the "culture of shamelessness" that has made it possible for the Abu Ghraib jailers to think such torture could be seen as "fun," as youthful hijinks to be shared with their peers, Sontag also recognizes that the impulse to hold onto photographic memories has its political uses. In a sense she has come to the opposite position from her initial dismay at the ubiquity of photographed images:

thanks to that fact, there is no way of keeping a lid on the record that indicts the brutalities of the American intervention in Iraq. "The pictures will not go away. That is the nature of the digital world in which we live" (ATST, 139).

To have been able to summon such rhetorical energy and intellectual fire for a just cause, a few months before her death, is remarkable and admirable. If there is a flaw in the essay, it is that she concentrates so fully on the torture-justifying remarks of Donald Rumsfeld and Rush Limbaugh, that the many articulate voices that were just as appalled, just as opposed to the war in Iraq as she was, go unacknowledged. It would seem that, for Sontag, in the last years of her life, Bush's America was the only America.

More on Politics

◫ It is sometimes erroneously thought that Sontag did an about-face regarding Soviet communism, but essentially she was a social democrat all along. You can find her writing as early as her 1963 essay on Camus, "I do not underestimate the courage involved in disavowing the pro-communism of many intellectuals in the late forties.

As a moral judgment, Camus' decision was right then, and since the death of Stalin he has been vindicated many times over in a political sense as well" (AI, 56). She drew the line early between Marxism (worthwhile) and Stalinism (vile). If she did alter her position, it was more of a slight verbal adjustment, which led her to abandon all future talk of the "Communist-humanist" and substitute the word "communism" for "Stalinism" in her controversial pronouncement, "communism is Fascism with a human face."

This dictum seemed to issue partly from a renewed sense of horror, during the eighties, at the revelations occasioned by Solzhenitsyn's *Gulag Archipelago*; there was much discussion in France at the time, led by Andre Glucksmann and others, comparing Stalin's atrocities with Hitler's. But Sontag's friendship with the anti-Soviet émigré poet Joseph Brodsky, whom she admired to the point of infatuation, may have been the more decisive influence. The sting in her aphorism came from the equation of communism with Fascism. For the most part, no one attempted to parse the other end of the sentence. What did she mean, communism had a human face? Was it intended as a partial exoneration of communism's mistakes? No, it was an ironic play on words, taking off from "Socialism with a human face," the liberalizing political program proposed by Alexander Dubcek in 1968 during the ill-fated Prague Spring. In effect, Sontag was again disparaging reformism as a useless strategy: one of her most consistent motifs.

As for myself, I did not understand at the time what the fuss was about. It seemed self-evident that Soviet communism had had some pretty disastrous consequences, and I thought it rather late in the game for Sontag to act as though she were saying something new, much less shocking. The brouhaha had less to do, I thought, with any re-interpretation of history than it did with certain social loyalties—whether it would give pain to one's Manhattan dinner-party companions to state the obvious, whether one would seem to be demeaning the blacklisted and the Rosenbergs by trashing Soviet Russia. It also had a good deal to do with Sontag's importance, or should I say her self-importance, as a public intellectual: if Joe Dokes or Chaim Yankel denounced Stalinism as a savage bloody business, who the hell cared? Not only did Sontag have the nerve to think it mattered what she said on the subject, she was actually right! Leftists of consequence did seem to care. They remembered it and held it against her like a scandal, and quoted the episode to each other when she died.

In her last decades she became, if anything, more politically committed—visited trouble spots, gave speeches about Bosnian suffering and other international causes—always, it seems to me, remaining, in the broadest sense, a supporter of the Left. Her putting on a production of *Waiting for Godot* for the besieged Sarajevans was certainly a good deed; she brought cultural support to many who felt abandoned. It would have been even more admirable if she had not been so self-congratulatory. She went about telling people that they could have no understanding of human suffering unless they went to Sarajevo. Not content to offer herself up as an exemplar of the politically engaged intellectual, she had to criticize other intellectuals for their cowardice, laziness, addiction to comfort, et cetera.* That was Sontag.

---

* In her 1995 essay "'There' and 'Here,'" she writes of "the morosely depoliticized intellectuals, with their cynicism always at the ready, their addiction to entertainment, their reluctance to inconvenience themselves for any cause, their devotion to personal safety. . . . (I can't count how many times I've been asked, each time I return to New York from Sarajevo, how I can go to a place that's so dangerous.)" (WSF, 328)

She reflected more and more on the public role of the intellectual, and the manifold temptations to pontificate. A writer, she said, has "the right to engage in debate on public matters, to make common cause and practice solidarity with like-minded others" but not "to produce opinions—moralistic sound-bites—on demand" (ATST, 150–51). "There is something vulgar about . . . mere opinion-mongering" (ATST, 153). She also argued that taking an open public stand on political matters was somehow at odds with being a writer, who is always courting ambiguity, and that going back and forth between these two identities (the privacy of a writer groping in the dark versus the assured public intellectual) meant leading a double life. She associated the privacy and primacy of the imagination with fiction writing, not essay writing, and as a consequence she sacralized fiction for its complexity and ambiguity. On the other hand, her social role in the literary life of Europe kept putting her in contact with political causes and pressing her to take a stand. Her dilemma was not so very different from that of every celebrated writer—Roth, Gordimer, Vargos-Llosa, Naipaul—of her generation.

The position she took in the end, I think, was the correct, reasonable one: that art must be kept separate from political persuasion, that the artist must retain his or her sovereignty to entertain any and all thoughts. What you did outside of art-making hours was another story. Burned by the experience of having been used to support causes that appeared dubious in retrospect, she came up with a sensible approach. "A good rule before one goes marching or signing anything: Whatever your tug of sympathy, you have no right to a public opinion unless you've been there, experienced firsthand and on the ground and for some considerable time the country, war, injustice, whatever, you are talking about. In the absence of such firsthand knowledge and experience: silence" (WSF, 298). This sage advice did not prevent her from saying, after 9/11, that the United States government was right to have invaded Afghanistan but not Iraq—even though she had never visited either Afghanistan or Iraq. As it is, the invasion of Afghanistan is also shaping up as an enormous mistake. I don't fault her particularly for having said that; many of us felt the same way about Afghanistan at the time. But it does show that she was not above the vulgarity of opinion-mongering, especially toward the end, when she obviously felt she had earned the right to pontificate.

On 9/11 and Television

Sontag's immediate response to the attacks on the World Trade Center and Pentagon, which appeared in the *New Yorker*, struck a raw nerve. At first she was severely criticized for her remarks, but now, especially in light of the Iraq War debacle, one is much more apt to hear her commended for her courage and foresight in resisting the mass-speak of American patriotism. Courage and outspokenness are virtues Sontag has always possessed. I must admit, though, that my own reaction to her initial statement about 9/11 was uneasy and somewhat critical. I agreed with her that it was incorrect to call the perpetrators "cowards," and that the attacks were connected to failures of American foreign policy, and I, too, was nauseated by what she called the "sanctimonious, reality-concealing rhetoric spouted by nearly all American officials and media commentators." But when she went on to say that that rhetoric "seems unworthy of a mature democracy" or that "Let's by all means grieve together. But let's not be stupid together," I cringed, feeling her timing was off—she was being insensitive. She seemed more eager to scold us for embarrassing her before her European intellectual friends who might think us immature than to appreciate why the stark horror of the attack might not be eliciting the most nuanced discourse. Perhaps the difference between us was that I'd been in Brooklyn that day and had seen the buildings go down, the ashes float across the East River, the acrid smell choking everyone, the thousands on foot crossing the Brooklyn Bridge, heard the worries of friends about whether their mates who worked downtown were alive, and so on, whereas Sontag was stuck in Berlin watching it all on TV.

As she acknowledged apologetically, and graciously, in "A Few Weeks Later," a follow-up piece, "Because I was in Berlin, where I had gone for ten days, my initial reaction to what was taking place was, literally, mediated." She "spent nearly all of the next forty-eight hours in front of the screen, mainly watching CNN, before returning to my laptop to dash off a diatribe against the inane and misleading demagoguery I had heard disseminated by American government and media figures." She admitted that after returning to New York and visiting Ground Zero, "the reality of the devastation, and the immensity of the loss of life, made my initial focus on the rhetoric surrounding the event seem to me less relevant." Good. Well said. She then went on instantly to add: "My consumption of reality via television had dropped to its usual level—zero. I have, stubbornly, never owned a TV set in America, although needless to say, I do watch TV when I am abroad." There is something priceless to me about this digression, which, in the midst of assessing the meaning of 9/11, assumes that we care about her TV-watching habits, and defensively clarifies that God forbid we should think her a couch potato, though of course she makes an exception for non-American television, which presumably is far superior to the home-grown brand, unless travel itself provokes a homesickness for inane American comforts that makes her lower her guard and indulge in the boob tube.

What made 9/11 especially horrifying was that she had to watch it on television.

Sontag never did "get" television. In *On Photography*, she pronounced, "Television is a stream of under-selected images, each of which cancels its predecessor" (OP, 18). Actually, it's quite selected, even if we don't always like the choices. In one of her last essays, "At the Same Time: The Novelist and Moral Reasoning," she wrote:

> The so-called stories that we are told on television satisfy our appetite for anecdote and offer us mutually canceling models of understanding. (This is reinforced by the practice of punc-

tuating television narratives with advertising.)
They implicitly affirm the idea that all information is potentially relevant (or "interesting"),
that all stories are endless—or if they do stop,
it is not because they have come to an end but,
rather, because they have been upstaged by
a fresher or more lurid or eccentric story. By
presenting us with a limitless number of non-
stopped stories, the narratives that the media
relate—the consumption of which has so dramatically cut into the time the educated public
once devoted to reading—offer a lesson of amorality and detachment that is antithetical to the
one embodied by the enterprise of the novel.
(ATST, 225)

This fancy-sounding, broad-brush accusation
that the medium is implicitly consumerist, and
therefore promotes amorality or detachment,
surely does not apply to television at its best,
such as *The Wire,* Fred Wiseman's incomparable documentaries, or the 1986 baseball playoffs
and World Series. Sontag praised *Berlin Alexanderplatz*, that great, serialized novel adaptation,
to the skies because it was by Fassbinder, which
seemingly excused the fact that it was made for
television. Her moral stance against television's

open-endedness, refusing to see that its series format encourages new forms of storytelling and character development, contradicted her customary approval of arduously protracted performances, from Wagner to Robert Wilson. Perhaps the reason is that we watch television in the comfort of our homes, undercutting in advance any claims to the rigorous, heroic endurance test or "ordeal" of prolonged art.

Greatness Besieged

In her later years Sontag became preoccupied with what she saw as the diminished possibilities of artistic greatness. The theme was first broached in her essay on Syberberg, in *Under the Sign of Saturn*:

> Lately, the appetite for the truly great work has become less robust. . . . Stripped of its heroic stature, of its claims as an adversary sensibility, modernism has proved acutely compatible with the ethos of an advanced consumer society. Art is now the name of a huge variety of satisfactions—of the unlimited proliferation, and devaluation, of satisfaction itself. Where

so many blandishments flourish, bringing off
a masterpiece seems a retrograde feat, a naïve
form of accomplishment. (137–38)

Some years later, she demands, "Is literary greatness still possible?" (WSF, 41) as the opening gam-
bit in her essay on W. G. Sebald, who seems to
fit the bill, solitarily, in her opinion. Writing on
the Polish poet Adam Zagajewski, she digresses
to say that communist regimes "embalmed the
old, hierarchical notions of achievement. . . . In
contrast, capitalism has a truly radical relation
to culture, dismantling the very notion of greatness in the arts, which is now most successfully
dismissed by the ecumenical philistinism of both
cultural progressives and cultural reactionaries
as an 'elitist' presumption." (WSF, 60).

Frankly, this whole notion that we no longer deserve to enter the Holy Land of great art
because we're debased entertainment-consum-
ers, and wouldn't know great art if it bit us on the
ass, strikes me as bunk. Many eras in the past had
audiences not particularly enlightened, yet great
art arose in their midst. Overall, I am not in the
habit of paying much attention to Sontag's jer-
emiads about consumer capitalism—not because
I don't agree that there is much to deplore in our

economic system, but because her critique is too broad: I don't learn from it; I get the sense of a pontificating jet-setter who doesn't really understand the nuts and bolts of global capitalism. But I'm less interested in disputing such views here than I am in trying to understand why she increasingly took the stand that greatness was a beleaguered, endangered species. Certainly it seems a departure from her optimistic celebration of the new artistic order in the sixties.

There is something very F. R. Leavis in this Great-Tradition attitude that an artist is either top-of-the-line or not worth considering. One could try to take Sontag's point of view and argue that with age came a commendable deepening of her standards; she now knew what great art was, and wanted it and only it. Or, one could surmise that with success came an increased snobbishness. In *Where the Stress Falls*, there begins to set in this habit of calling attention to her social circle, her friendship with luminaries, who make up a more or less exclusive aristocracy. No longer is she on her knees to the greats of the past and present; now she wants it known that she is on an equal footing with her subjects. She namedrops her friendship with Brodsky, Baryshnikov, Lucinda Child, Avedon, Juan Rolfo, Mapplethorpe, Hodgkin, Danilo Kis, Elizabeth Hardwick.* With this "A list" comes the assertion that genius is rare, and only the highest standards count.

In *Where the Stress Falls*, Sontag's intelligence is still dazzling, with astute insights about literature, dance, opera, photography, film, music, painting, but now there is more of an emphasis on exclusion. The reader is not particularly courted, not even wanted; what is wanted is her circle of accomplished friends. "One should write to please not one's contemporaries but one's predecessors, Brodsky often declared" (WSF, 331). Indeed, it would seem as if the Nobel Prize–winning Brodsky, whom she eulogized in this fourth collection, had succeeded Roland Barthes in the eighties as her main inspiration, not always with happy results: she took on some of his Cold War

---

* Examples: "each time I've congratulated a friend or acquaintance who is a dancer on a superb performance—and I include Baryshnikov . . ." (WSF, 189); "I've had the privilege of being a friend of Danilo Kis" (WSF, 96); Robert Mapplethorpe is "a photographer I intensely admire (who is also a friend)" (WSF, 235); she writes paeans to her friend, the painter Howard Hodgkin and acrostics to the dancer Lucinda Child; she gets to honor "the promise I made to Juan Rolfo when we met in Buenos Aires shortly before his death that *Pedro Páramo* would appear in an accurate and uncut edition" (WSF, 108).

truculence, as well as his conviction that poetry was Queen of the arts, to be practiced correctly only by a tiny cadre of the anointed.

Sontag had a hero-worshipping tendency, the need to admire only the finest, side by side with her inclination to dismiss everything else. The last speaker in *The Volcano Lover*, the martyred patriot Eleonora de Fonseca Pimentel, says about Emma Hamilton: "She was an enthusiast, and would have enlisted herself with the same ardor in the cause of whomever she loved. I can easily imagine Emma Hamilton, had her nationality been different, as a republican heroine, who might have ended most courageously at the foot of some gallows. That is the nullity of women like her." In this harsh judgment of her heroine, I hear a touch of self-appraisal, especially when Sontag assigns the term "enthusiasm" (one of her favorite self-characterizations) to Emma. She also identified with Eleonora, the woman-denying part of herself, who said: "Sometimes I had to forget that I was a woman to accomplish the best of which I was capable. Or I would lie to myself about how complicated it is to be a woman. Thus do all women, including the author of this book." A postmodern novelist cannot get any more self-reflexive than that. It is important to remember that the speaker, the dead Eleonora, ends the novel with these words: "But I cannot forgive those who did not care about more than their own glory or well-being. They were despicable. Damn them all." That is the dismissive side of Sontag, which in this case has the final word.

In the essays which make up her last, posthumous essay collection, *At the Same Time*, Sontag's preoccupation with greatness grew into an almost manic tic. As one otherwise favorable reviewer, Jonathan Rees, put it: "She finds it hard to talk about writers without telling us who is or is not 'great' or 'supremely great,' as if world literature were a competitive sport, and she the ultimate umpire."

"Standards" becomes her rallying cry. Sontag saw herself at the end as standing virtually alone, defending the only criterion that mattered: "The greatest offense now, in matters both of the arts and of culture generally, not to mention political life, is to seem to be upholding some better, some exigent standard, which is attacked, both from the left and the right, as either naïve or (a new banner for the philistines) 'elitist.'" (ATST, 219). She was no longer in sync with contemporary culture, but proud to be called an elitist, standing above the fray and judging it worthless mass-think, save for a handful of enthusiastic exceptions.

Illness and Death

▣ In her 1980 essay on Elias Canetti, "Mind and Passion," which concluded *Under the Sign of Saturn*, she wrote: "To protest against power, power as such; to protest against death (he was one of the great death-haters of literature)—these are broad targets, rather invincible enemies" (USS, 192). Sontag was herself one of the great death-haters; we know from her son's and others' testimony how strong was her avidity for longevity, how little willing she was to "go gentle into that good night." She valiantly battled full-blown cancer three times, the first two times regaining her health.

In 1975 Sontag was diagnosed with breast cancer and told by her doctors that she had only a ten percent chance of living beyond two years. She chose to have a radical mastectomy and to undergo thirty months of chemotherapy. Sontag came to spend a long time in the Kingdom of Illness, experiencing it, fighting it, writing about it. It was a measure of her suitability for the literary vocation that, whatever difficulty life threw at her, she accepted as a challenge and turned into subject matter.

Illness as Metaphor appeared first in 1978 as a three-part series in the *New York Review of Books*, and later that same year as a small volume on its own. Her purpose was to be of use to other cancer-sufferers who had been made to feel shame and humiliation, and indeed, this little book gave comfort to many thousands of patients and their families. In keeping with its utilitarian intent, the writing style was lucid and accessible, purged of that teasing, mystifying opacity that had characterized her earlier books.

In examining the life-work of any writer, it is instructive to consider which themes, positions, or stylistic maneuvers are carried forth from the past, which ones abandoned or reversed—in other words, how the writer builds on infrastructural footfalls he or she knows can be relied on, even as the new challenge is embraced. So, just as in *Against Interpretation*, *Illness as Metaphor* advocates a prophylactic stance against one form of rhetoric; as in *On Photography*, it rummages far and wide through the literature, accumulating a commonplace book's worth of quotations on the subject; it indicts psychology and America; it corrects hyperbole in a previous work;[*] it resists a personal approach. If *On Photography* called for

---

[*] "D. H. Lawrence once called masturbation 'the deepest and most dangerous cancer of our civilization'; and I once wrote, in the heat of despair over America's war on Vietnam, that 'the white race is the cancer of human history'" (IAM, 84).

an ecology of images, this succeeding book calls for a conservation of metaphors. (What *was* this legislative urge in her to control or to purify a seemingly random, unstoppable flow?)

The argument of *Illness as Metaphor* is a fairly simple one: the metaphors that are used to describe illness, or to describe other social problems (such as urban decay) in terms of illness, end up stigmatizing those who are stricken. "My point is that illness is *not* a metaphor, and that the most truthful way of regarding illness—and the healthiest way of being ill—is one most purified of, most resistant to, metaphoric thinking" (IAM, 3).

That it is impossible to purify the mind of metaphor is an argument she addresses in her book on AIDS—though not in this one, since, as we have seen, she does not like to dilute the force of a polemic by arguing against herself in the same work. In that later book, she will say, "Of course one cannot think without metaphors. But that doesn't mean there aren't some metaphors we might well abstain from or try to retire" (AAIM, 93). There is still the need to ask whether the metaphors she wants to retire are really so destructive. The skepticism she faces from some readers is: What can be so harmful in a metaphor? In a world that holds so many larger terrors and evils, surely a fanciful comparison between one thing and another, however inexact, cannot matter so.

Her real enemy, it turns out, is actually not metaphorical thinking, but speculation that there is a certain personality type susceptible to one sort of illness or another. For instance: the hypothesis that those who repress their anger and sexuality stand a better chance of getting cancer (an insulting idea she traces from Norman Mailer back to the psychologists Wilhelm Reich and Georg Groddeck), while those who are passionate or spiritually ethereal may incline to tuberculosis. As she states, bluntly and eloquently:

> Psychological theories of illness are a powerful means of placing the blame on the ill. Patients who are instructed that they have, unwittingly, caused their disease are also being made to feel that they have deserved it. . . . Such preposterous and dangerous views manage to put the onus of the disease on the patient and not only weaken the patient's ability to understand the range of plausible medical treatment but also, implicitly, direct the patient away from such treatment. (IAM, 57, 47)

A sensible, worthwhile, humane position. As usual, however, she overshoots the mark with sweeping statements such as: "Theories that diseases are caused by mental states and can be cured by will power are always an index of how much is not understood about the physical terrain of illness" (IAM, 55). Maybe will power cannot do much against disease, though some anecdotal evidence suggests otherwise. The jury is still out, however, on the intricate relationship between psyche and soma.

There are other distortions: by making Wilhelm Reich into the heavy ("Reich, who did more than anyone else to disseminate the psychological theory of cancer"), she wildly overstates his influence, since he was dismissed by many people as a crackpot and died in a federal prison. Moreover, I still find it hard to see what is so bad about using military metaphors, such as waging war on cancer, if it will help to mobilize society's resources.

Sontag's distaste for consumerist America leads her to conclude in the stern voice of a social critic (her weakest, windiest manner):

Our views about cancer, and the metaphors we have imposed on it, are so much a vehicle for the large insufficiencies of this culture: for our shallow attitude toward death, for our anxieties about feeling, for our reckless improvident responses to our real "problems of growth," for our inability to construct an advanced industrial society that properly regulates consumption, and for our justified fears of the increasingly violent course of history. (IAM, 87)

Here it seems that she is coming dangerously close to equating our horror of cancer, metaphorically speaking, with shallow America, a way for her to side-step instead of acknowledge the very real, very appropriate sorrow, rage, horror, and grief the illness arouses.

Still, if Sontag does not always clinch her argument, she has at least stirred up the ground in a suggestive, innovative manner. She draws out well a comparison between tuberculosis and cancer, the former romanticized as both ethereal and sexual, the latter stubbornly resisting glamorization. She brings in entertaining references to Kafka, Mann, Dickens, Freud, Auden, Blake, Kant, Hugo, Homer, Ibsen, Keats, Byron, Stevenson, Stowe, Baudelaire, Tolstoy, and the Goncourt Brothers. And her passion, or, as she would later call it, her "evangelical zeal," continues to make this one of her most endearing works. She took on the activist role here, avoiding that of personal witness or victim. Her suppressing any mention of autobiographical connection—that she herself had had cancer—infused the little book with an even more mysterious urgency.

She begins *AIDS and Its Metaphors*, some twelve years later, by addressing directly this absence in the previous book on illness: "I didn't think it would be useful—and I wanted to be useful—to tell yet one more story in the first person of how someone learned that she or he had cancer, wept, struggled, was comforted, suffered, took courage . . . though mine was also that story. A narrative, it seemed to me, would be less useful than an idea" (AAIM, 101).

But *AIDS and Its Metaphors* is a more tired, obligatory book than its predecessor, and feels at times like the mechanical extension of a franchise. Once again, she surveys the literature for destructive metaphors, the most dominant one being "plague," which ostensibly fosters a defeatist attitude of "inexorability, inescapability." As she has less of an historical literature to sift through, the discovery of the disease being relatively new, her discourse fastens on current attitudes and prejudices. Sontag's role is again that of advocate, this time for the homosexual community, who have been stigmatized with the ugly notion that AIDS is "a punishment for deviant sex" (AAIM, 151). Her arguments against blaming the victim are not only persuasive but compassionate and just. It is only when she tries to navigate the complexities of AIDS prevention that she begins to trip over inner contradictions. Warning that we are "in the early stages of a sexual depression" (AAIM, 164), she blames, as usual, that ever-available if vague target, capitalist consumer culture:

> Given the imperatives about consumption and the virtually unquestioned value attached to the expression of self, how could sexuality *not* have come to be, for some, a consumer option: an exercise of liberty, of increased mobility, of the pushing back of limits. Hardly an invention of the male homosexual subculture, recreational, risk-free sexuality is an inevitable reinvention of the culture of capitalism, and was guaranteed by medicine as well. The advent of AIDS seems to have changed all that, irrevocably. (AAIM, 165)

Sontag seems unsure for a moment whether to play the ascetic or the aesthete: to lament the excesses of consumer capitalism or the loss of the sixties dream of sexual libertinism. She comes down on the aesthete side, with a caveat against monogamous sexual prudence that ties together all her long-held artistic positions:

> The behavior AIDS is stimulating is part of a larger grateful return to what is perceived as "conventions," like the return to figure and landscape, tonality and melody, plot and character, and other much-vaunted repudiations of difficult modernism in the arts. The reduction in the imperative of promiscuity in the middle class, a growth of the ideal of monogamy, of a prudent sexual life, is as marked in, say, Stockholm, with its tiny number of AIDS cases, as it is in New York, where the disease can accurately be called of epidemic proportions. The response to AIDS, while in part perfectly rational, amplifies a widespread questioning that had been rising in intensity throughout the 1970s of many of the ideals (and risks) of enlightened modernity; and the new sexual realism goes with the rediscovery of the joys of tonal music, Bouguereau, a career in investment banking, and church weddings. (AAIM, 166–67)

This is undoubtedly one of the silliest passages Sontag ever wrote, not least because she suddenly goes tone-deaf to the immeasurable suffering AIDS has caused, compared to the risk of diluting "difficult modernism in the arts." She has the nerve to saddle those who would reduce that disease's risks through safe sex or fidelity with the accusation of bad taste, of preferring pretty, hummable music to atonality, landscapes to abstract art—in short, of embracing bourgeois comfort. Never mind that it is possible to like both tonal and atonal music, or to be married in a church and enjoy Bresson, or to be a freelance, starving bohemian and still monogamous.

Sontag did a better job at registering the exact tones of communal grief and consolation provoked by AIDS in her celebrated short story "The Way We Live Now." The piece is at once an "unbroken monologue" of the sort Nathalie Sarraute had advocated, and a choral channeling of at least a dozen voices. It consists of unbroken paragraph blocks that go on for pages, each section separated by a white double-space. One section begins, for instance:

And when, not right away but still only three weeks later, he was accepted into the protocol for the new drug, which took considerable behind-the-scenes lobbying with the doctors, he talked less about being ill, according to Donny, which seemed like a good sign, Kate felt, a sign that he was not feeling like a victim, feeling not that he *had* a disease but, rather, was living *with* a disease (that was the right cliché, wasn't it), a more hospitable arrangement, said Jan, a kind of cohabitation which implied that it was something temporary, that could be terminated, but terminated how, said Hilda, and when you say hospitable, Jan, I hear hospital. (TWWLN, 18)

Here we see the multiple hand-offs from one narrative viewpoint to another within the context of one long, run-on sentence. The lengthy sentence is a favorite device of modernist novelists Sontag most appreciated, from Henry James (whose qualifying tone she seems to mimic here) to Proust and Musil, through Bernhard, Sebald, Saramago, and Tsypkin.* The effect of the technique in this

---

*In her essay, "Loving Dostoyevsky," on Leonid Tsypkin, she wrote: "Tsypkin's sentences call to mind Jose Saramago's run-on sentences, which fold dialogue into description and description into dialogue, and are spiked by verbs that refuse to stay consistently in either the past or the present tense. In their incessantness, Tsypkin's sentences have something of the same force and hectic authority as those of Thomas Bernhard. . . . His prose is an ideal vehicle for the emotional intensity and abundance of his subject. In a relatively short book, the long sentence bespeaks inclusiveness and associativeness, the passionate agility of a temperament steeped, in most respects, in adamancy" (ATST, 35–36).

particular story is to blend many voices into a hydra-headed spokesperson, thereby conveying the collective community of AIDS sufferers and care-givers—friends, acquaintances, relatives—who gather around them. The individual is not as important as the epochal consciousness that arises in the face of the traumatic disease. In that way, the "idea" again takes precedence over the "story" of one person who learned he or she had the illness, et cetera.

What exactly is the idea in "The Way We Live Now"? I would say it is an examination of the relationship between individual identity and group affinity at the end of the twentieth century, with AIDS as the catalyst. Illness leads to depersonalization, but it also fosters collectivity, as a sort of political side-benefit. It promotes tenderness and responsibility for each other, as well as a group-mind that takes consolation in cliché. I don't think Sontag herself meant the story to be reassuring, in that triumph-of-the-human-spirit way. If anything, readers might finish it, as I did, with a chilly sense of the degree to which one is always alone, in illness and death, for all the good intentions of others.

That isolation puts me in mind of the photographs Annie Leibovitz took of Susan Sontag, looking ravished on her sickbed in the hospital, and then a stiff block on the funeral bier. I have to say that I don't like those photographs. It's not just that they are opportunistic—I could forgive that if they were great images—but that they're mediocre photographs, not insightful, not artfully composed, *and* on top of that, opportunistic. The Sontag who appreciated only the finest photography deserved better.

Then again, Sontag submitted, while she was alive, to posing for Liebovitz and allowing candid photographs to be taken of her in sickness and in health. Snapshots have never been Liebovitz's forte—where she excels is the carefully composed studio shot, with lighting technicians and hair stylists, the *Vanity Fair* cover—but some of her snapshots of Sontag, embarking or disembarking en route to somewhere, with a look of exhaustion held under restraint, waiting for enthusiasm to kick in, have a sorrowful elegance that is very moving. The famous description of the poet Pasternak's face—a man and his horse—comes to mind. Sontag rode herself, her talent and her destiny, hard, and as far as they would take her.

Writers, however honest, do all they can to control what the public thinks of them, by shaping and standing guard over their texts; by reclusively refusing to be photographed or by seeking the limelight: some, like Sontag, going to extremes to invent a persona that is much more mannered and mandarin than their beginnings would suggest. (Similarly, Brooklyn-raised Lionel Trilling, with his vaguely Anglican accent.) But in the end they are at the mercy of the scatterbrained world's opinion: an often humiliating, distracted, or insolent opinion, be it the result of photographers at their deathbed or biographers and critics who try to take their measure after they are gone. The best they can hope for is that they continue to be read (as surely Susan Sontag will), enjoying, if they can in the afterlife, what accumulated slivers of insight may accrue from that shaggy, communal critical process.

▣ ACKNOWLEDGMENTS

This book is dedicated to David Shapiro, extraordinary poet, whose friendship and wise counsel have done much to sustain me in this effort.

I would also like to thank my editor, Hanne Winarsky, who initiated the project and made many useful suggestions, and my ever-trusty agent, Wendy Weil. Gretl Claggett, my Goucher intern who located many documents from the library, was a godsend. Deep gratitude to my wife, Cheryl, and to the following friends for reading the manuscript and helping me develop the ideas in it: Max Apple, Carmen Boullosa, James Harvey, Elizabeth Kendall, Max Kozloff, Jonathan Lethem, Carrie Rickey, Vijay Seshadri, Mark Street, and Benjamin Taylor.